MEMOIRS OF
EIGHTEENTH-CENTURY FOOTMAN

John Macdonald (1741–96) was born, and died, a Scottish High-lander, a native of Inverness-shire. First published at the time of the French Revolution, these memoirs of his days in service have come to light again—giving us a delicious opportunity to savour the stories gleaned from his years of travelling the world. From the palaces of the Indian princes in Bombay, to the Court of Louis XV at Versailles, Macdonald served as valet, footman and hairdresser to at least twenty-seven different masters, who were usually capricious members of the nobility, and who included James Coutts the banker.

In 1768, as the result of an errand, it fell to Macdonald to witness the deathbed of Laurence Sterne—surely his soulmate, for both saw life through "Shandyesque" spectacles. "Beau Macdonald" also goes down in history as the pioneer of the use of the umbrella in London, at a time when it was regarded as "foreign" in England.

Irresistible to women, and popular with men, the spell of John Macdonald remains strong to this day. His memoirs are introduced in this edition by Peter Quennell, for many years the co-editor of *History Today* and also a distinguished and prolific literary critic, biographer and essayist.

MEMOIRS OF AN EIGHTEENTH-CENTURY FOOTMAN

John Macdonald
(1745–1779)

INTRODUCTION BY
Peter Quennell

CENTURY PUBLISHING
LONDON

First published in Great Britain in 1790 by John Forbes
This edition published in 1985 by
Century Hutchinson Ltd,
Portland House, 12–13 Greek Street,
London W1V 5LE

ISBN 0 7126 0992 X

*The cover shows a detail from 'The Countess's Morning Levée'
by William Hogarth, in the National Gallery, London*

Reprinted in Great Britain by
Richard Clay (The Chaucer Press) Ltd, Bungay, Suffolk

TRAVELS,

IN VARIOUS PARTS OF

EUROPE, ASIA, AND AFRICA,

DURING A SERIES OF THIRTY YEARS AND UPWARDS.

BY

JOHN <u>*MACDONALD*</u>,

A CADET OF THE FAMILY OF KEPPOCH

IN

INVERNESS-SHIRE;

WHO,

After the Ruin of his Family in 1745, was thrown when a Child on the wide World; the Ways of which, with many curious, useful, and interesting Particulars he had occasion to observe, and has taken care, by Means of a regular Journal, to record, while he served, in various departments, a great number of Noblemen and Gentlemen, English, Scotch, Irish, Dutch, &c. &c.

LONDON:

PRINTED FOR THE AUTHOR,
AND SOLD BY J. FORBES, COVENT-GARDEN.
MDCCXC.

INTRODUCTION

On the afternoon of March 18, 1768 a large dinner-party of gentlemen, among whom were Hume, Garrick and the rakish Lord March, the future Duke of Queensberry, heard that the celebrated novelist Laurence Sterne—their "very great favourite"—was lying seriously ill above "the silk-bag shop in Old Bond Street": and one of them ordered his footman to go and enquire "how Mr Sterne is today". The footman's name was John Macdonald—and a book that he published many years later contains a strangely vivid account of poor Yorick's dreadful passing. Macdonald had gone to the silk-bag shop, and he reported:

"The mistress opened the door . . . She told me to go up to the nurse. I went into the room, and he was just a-dying. I waited ten minutes; but in five he said, '*Now it is come*'. He put up his hand as if to stop a blow, and died . . ."

This admirable piece of descriptive prose has been quoted by all Laurence Sterne's biographers with the exception of Sir Walter Scott. Otherwise, the book that Macdonald produced in 1790 attracted very little notice; and it was not reprinted until 1927, when it found its way into a series of travel books, and was edited and introduced by John Beresford, an unusually perceptive man of letters, who also discovered Woodforde's *Diary of a Country Parson*. During the Victorian Age, apart from Sterne's bio-

INTRODUCTION

graphers, the only writer to mention Macdonald's work was Lecky, the historian of eighteenth-century England. In 1892, besides praising this "curious autobiography", he cited one or two extracts.

Like William Hickey's splendid *Memoirs*, which cover much the same period—Hickey entered the world in 1749; Macdonald, in 1741—the Scotsman's fascinating narrative was the product of an un-tutored story-teller. Indeed Macdonald was consider-ably the less experienced; for whereas Hickey's father had been a friend of Samuel Johnson and he himself, though an incurably idle youth, had re-ceived his education at an English public school, Macdonald was the offspring of a hard-pressed Highland cattle farmer. After the disastrous Battle of Culloden, at which their father fell or vanished, John and his sister Kitty and two of their three brothers had become bare-footed vagrants. Headed by the valiant fourteen-year-old girl, they left home and walked in the space of two months from Inver-ness to Edinburgh, a journey of "one hundred and fifty measured miles".

Arrived in Edinburgh, they lived on charity, and slept in an empty lumber-room under some ancient blankets. But John, while he wandered around the city, picked up many useful bits of knowledge. Since he loved horses and passed much of his time with grooms, postilions and coachmen, he learned the niceties of riding and driving, and studied the con-struction of an eighteenth-century carriage, so that in later life, should a sudden breakdown occur, he

could always repair a trace or mend a wheel. He was
neither an unhappy nor often a hungry boy. He was
not ashamed to beg and readily accepted tips, and at
that time, "a working-man could dine well for two-
pence", he records.

He had, moreover, very important assets—a mus-
cular body and an extremely handsome face. Of
these gifts he soon made good use and, once he had
nearly grown up and begun to earn a few guineas,
he further improved his appearance by purchasing
fashionable clothes and cultivating gentlemanly
manners. "I delighted in dress and powder," he
tells us. "My name was commonly the French Macdonald." Ladies, he noticed, cast him appreciative
glances. "What makes the women take to me so?"
he asked his old friend Mrs Bell. She had already
warned him that women would be his ruin if he
didn't take care; and "Johnny," she then added,
"there is nothing further in it than this—they think
you have so good a temper, and never hear you say
an ill word; and you are so obliging in your
way . . .".

His charm and willingness to oblige continued to
distinguish Macdonald. His was an equable and
easy-going character. Although he admired the
pomp and gaiety of the Anglo-Scottish upper
classes, he did not spitefully envy them or fret
against his own subordinate position, but, as he
watched their extravagant balls and picnics, resolved
that he would share their fun. His real metier,
he quickly decided, was that of a professional

gentleman's servant. He had all the necessary qualifications and, when he was nineteen and remarkably advanced for his years, he joined the household of his first employer.

True, Mr Gibb was a prosperous businessman; but Macdonald presently moved on to the service of a patrician landowner, John Hamilton of Bargeny, who had married the daughter of a Scottish earl, and was next engaged by Lord Crauford, whose style of life proved equally magnificent: "we had four fine long-tailed greys . . . Our liveries were blue and scarlet trimmed with gold lace". Altogether John Macdonald served no less than twenty-seven employers and, as a rule, he enjoyed their company and tolerated their varying moods and whims; even though one choleric gentleman broke a billiard cue across his back.

The details of Macdonald's professional career will interest every student of the period. By modern standards, his wages were low—fourteen shillings a week; twenty guineas a year; fifteen guineas a year and half-a-guinea a week; seventeen guineas a year and a livery; and, at length, forty guineas a year, provided he would accompany Colonel Dow to Hindustan. But his perquisites, no doubt, were numerous—Macdonald seems to have been a shrewd economist; and a resplendent cast-off suit, richly embroidered and laced, was occasionally thrown in. For such rewards and free board and lodging, he performed a multiplicity of tasks. Having brought the gentleman's breakfast, Mac-

INTRODUCTION

donald was both the valet who helped him put on his
clothes and the barber—another self-taught rôle—
who expertly "dressed" his hair, applying just the
right amount of pomatum and delicately rolling up
the loosened curls. Later in the day, he might wait at
table, jog, bearing messages, around the country, or
display his talents as a cook. Macdonald's culinary
chef-d'œuvre, which was frequently applauded by
foreigners if he and his gentleman happened to be
travelling abroad, he called "the Queen of Scots
soup". He gives us the recipe. It required "six
chickens cut in small pieces", eight eggs beaten up
with their whites, and large quantities of salt and
cayenne pepper.

The personal aspects of Macdonald's autobiography are as interesting and revealing. Like Hickey
again, he loved and pursued women and twice, at an
early stage of his career, he forfeited a good post
because an employer suspected—possibly with some
reason—that his wife was growing far too fond of
John. When he heard that matrimonial differences
had arisen in the Hamilton and Crauford families—
in each the lady had left her husband, and it was said
that he had been the cause—he admitted that the
rumour might conceivably have some foundation.
"Master John," his fellow servants informed him,
"the ladies say you are not a proper person to live
where there are married people"; and thereafter, he
wisely concluded, he had better work for single
gentlemen.

Macdonald's descriptions of his love-affairs are

generally brief, but sometimes oddly moving. He was an adventurous, maybe an unscrupulous amorist; but it is clear he did not lack a heart. The story of Amelia Burn, Lady Crauford's chambermaid and "the handsomest girl in the parish or the shire", has an especially pathetic close: "From the first day," he writes, "Amelia took a liking to me and I to her"; and, just at the time Lord Crauford abruptly dismissed him, he learned that she was with child. "I thought to marry her when I got a place," he declares; and meanwhile, he hired her a room near her mother's house, "gave her six guineas, and other things necessary", and arranged that the child should have a decent christening. He himself must look for a place in Edinburgh, and set off again upon his travels. Another servant accompanied him:

". . . Amelia went a little way with us. He asked her if she would like to have John Macdonald for a husband. She answered she would wait twenty years and then beg her bread with me for life."

Later, he returned with his previous employer Mr Hamilton, who appears to have forgiven his past offences, and whom he had temporarily rejoined. "Have you not a child in this parish?" Mr Hamilton enquired as they caught sight of a neighbouring castle, and, Macdonald having agreed that he had, remarked "Well, you may go and see him: I shall' ride gently on". Thus Macdonald was able to visit and console Amelia, and make his unknown son's acquaintance; after which he obeyed the call of duty and next morning rode away again. There the story ends; but to assume from his desertion of Amelia and their boy that he had a cold and coarse-grained nature would, I believe, be totally misguided.

His *Travels*, the book that he published at his own expense when he was forty-nine, despite his obvious shortcomings (of which the worst was vanity), is a sympathetic self-portrait and reflects not only his courage and enterprise and fiercely independent spirit, but also his sensitiveness to natural beauty, as shown in his descriptions of the sumptuous Indian landscapes he had observed while journeying with Colonel Dow. He had also a natural taste for music. Near Aix-la-Chapelle, he recollects, "the shepherd-boys meet in the evenings and play on the German flute, which makes it very agreeable as you ride along the road".

Travelling was Macdonald's passion. "No king in the world," he writes of one jaunt, "could have enjoyed more pleasure than we did by going from place to place"; and his last pages chronicle an expedition to Spain that changed the course of his existence. He had paid an earlier visit to the city, and now discovered that a local inn-keeper's daughter had recently borne a child whom her neighbours dubbed "the little Englishman". Malilia was eighteen; he was thirty-eight. It was time, he felt, to settle down. The inn-keeper and his family then welcomed him with open arms; tears were shed; Malilia embraced him and collapsed in a dead faint: "I sent for a priest, and was married directly." Beyond that point we cannot follow him. "So now," he concludes, "I end the history of my travels", and thereafter disappears.

No one can tell us if he still has Spanish descendants, or whether he prospered as a citizen of Toledo. We learn, nevertheless, that he could not afford to retire, and soon found employment that suited him at the Hotel de Naples with a certain Mr Logaro. I like to think that eventually he became the proprietor of the hotel himself; and I imagine him sitting in the garden or the bar, telling stories of his English youth—how he had watched poor Yorick die and, perhaps an even more remarkable experience, had been the first pedestrian brave and farsighted enough to carry an umbrella through the streets of London.

Peter Quennell
1985

The dates are approximate, as the servant was not always precise, though quite sufficiently precise for ordinary purposes. Here is the list:

1. Mr Gibb of Edinburgh, Proprietor of Livery Stables: 1746-50.
2. John Hamilton, Esq., of Bargeny: 1750-6.
3. The Earl of Crauford: 1756-9.
4. John Hamilton—a second time—: 1760-1.
5. Colonel Skene: 1761.
6. Major Joass: 1761-3.
7. Major Libellier: 1763.
8. Major Deibbeige: 1763-4.
9. Mr Ferguson (brother to Sir Adam Ferguson) and Mr Creighton
10. A Kentish Powder Merchant (unnamed) } 1764-5?
11. Mr Campbell, brother of Mr Campbell of Shawfield
12. Mr John Crauford of Errol: 1765?-8.
13. Colonel Alexander Dow, first time for a few months in 1768.
14. The Hon. Keith Stewart: 1768-9.
15. Colonel Dow, second time: 1769-71.
16. Colonel Keating: 1771-2.
17. Mr Shaw, of the East India Company's service: 1772.
18. Captain Thomas Taylor, of the *Hampshire*, on the way back from India: 1772-3.
19. James Nowland
20. Mr Lecall
21. Mr Dawson of Dublin
22. Mr Brown   } 1773-4
23. Mr Freeman of the Inner Temple
24. Mr Lowrie
25 Mr George Spencer, Madeira Merchant

NOTES

26. James Macpherson, Esq., the eminent "Ossian", Historian, and Man of Letters: 1774.

27. James Coutts, Banker: 1774-6 ?

28. Sir John Stuart, of Allan Bank, Co. Berwick: 1776-8 ; in point of fact he was not yet Sir John, but was the eldest son and heir to the Baronetcy to which he succeeded in 1796.

29. James O'Neil, Esq., of Dublin, a rich young Wine Merchant: 1778-9.

PREFACE

TO THE EDITION OF 1790

THE following pages, the production of a candid, though uncultivated, mind, show how much it is in the power of natural simplicity and good sense to make their way to the heart, without the lessons of the schools and the aid of artificial composition. The author relates the catastrophe of his family, the various accidents that befell himself, and the observations which he had occasion to make on a great variety of places, objects, and characters, with an air of truth and sincerity, which gains a more ready and firmer belief, and takes faster hold of the mind and heart, than narratives seasoned with profound reflections and composed with the greatest care and artifice. He never, as he honestly declares, " takes his own part ". He seems always to speak from the bottom of his soul ; he confesses, on every occasion, his own weakness or folly. The simple strokes of truth and nature with which he paints the caprices, the vanities and vices of others, possess all the force of satire ; and the attentive and enlightened reader finds a gratification in observing how objects strike a sound and sensible mind, free from all system and prejudice of education ; for our untutored traveller, cast on the wide world, an orphan of only five years of age, learned to read and write, and cast up accounts, merely by his own application and industry.

I

PREFACE

Placed in a vast variety of situations and departments, in the service of a great variety of persons of rank and fortune, he had an opportunity of contemplating both high and low life, of becoming acquainted with the ways of the world, and of treasuring up, as he has done in the Journal of his life, many anecdotes and remarks interesting and useful both to masters and servants.—If John Macdonald professes not the learning and the wit of Gil Blas, he draws more from truth and nature; and he has had, though in a humbler sphere, almost as many adventures. Another circumstance, not to be omitted in an apology for the publication of these travels, is, that their author, mindful of the helpless state of his infancy, embraces every occasion of illustrating the beneficence of an all-ruling Providence. This, indeed, may be considered as forming, in some measure, the principle by which he connects the various incidents of his life.

These are the remarks of the Editor to whom Mr Macdonald committed his manuscript for the purpose of correcting and improving his style; but who judged it unnecessary, and even improper, to make any other alterations therein than a few that seemed here and there necessary, in order to render it intelligible.

The Life and Travels of John Macdonald

IT was formerly customary for the younger sons of gentlemen's families, in Scotland, that did not go into the navy or army to become graziers. My father, who had no estate of his own, rented near a thousand acres of the Laird of Grant. He reared cattle, and drove them to the South of Scotland, and into England, where he sold them. He married, at the age of twenty, a daughter of some family of the name of Mackay; but I never knew anything of her family. My mother bore a daughter to him, and four sons; but he, being a rover in disposition and always hankering after the army, addicted himself to the use of the broadsword, in which he excelled; and, being very hot and quarrelsome, challenged and fought many gentlemen with the sword and target, which affronted many families in the neighbourhood, and broke my mother's heart.

I was born in the beginning of the year 1741; and, about two years after, my mother had another son, of whom she died in child-bed. On this my father was almost distracted, swore he would never marry another woman, and said often to the children: " Thy mother I shall never forget." Then he turned

extravagant, did not ſtay at home so much as he
should have done, but neglected his business; and
when the Rebellion began, in 1745, he raised a number
of men of his own name, whom he employed as his
drovers, and marched them up to Prince Charles,
whose firſt camp was about twenty miles off my
father's house. The Prince received him very kindly,
and made him a captain of the Macdonald's clan. He
then left his business to the grieve, or foreman, and
very seldom came home. He was in all the battles
that ensued in Scotland, till he fell at Culloden.
Having thus given an account of my parentage, I shall
go on with perfect impartiality; and, without taking
my own part, to relate every thing that I did, or
suffered, whether good or bad.

The Laird of Grant, thinking things would go
wrong with Prince Charles, took possession of what
cattle was left, and put a person in the house in his
name, which indeed saved it afterwards from the
flames, when the rebels' horses were burnt in their
ſtables. The man that had the charge of my father's
affairs went with the cattle, and had a place at the
Laird of Grant's. His name was Boyd. He took my
eldeſt brother, as he had a great regard for the boy
and the boy for him, and then we four were left with
the maid, who took no care of the house or any little
things that were left, as she never expected any wages;
but soon went off with a lover. We were now left
alone; but my siſter being by the providence of

God bold, of a heroic disposition, and strong withal, was prepared to go through the following hardships.— Boyd, having read a letter dated from my father, Captain Macdonald, at Goolen's Inn and Livery Stables, Head of the Canongate, Edinburgh, an answer was returned; but I believe all the letters to Prince Charles's camp were intercepted, for we never saw or heard from our father more.

After the letter came from our father, my sister was never easy, but going from one town to another, on foot, sometimes to Inverness, then to see my brother, out and in, to and fro. This made the people take notice and say she had something extraordinary to go through. Now we had no person with us in the house; but the neighbours came to see us now and then. My sister had it in her head to go to Edinburgh, to see my father. She got all the money she could get together, which was fourteen pounds Scots, or twenty-three shillings and four-pence English. With this, the letter from my father in her bosom, and her three brothers in her hand, out she sets for Edinburgh, from the parish of Urquhart, about the middle of September, 1745. Now our ages were as follows: Kitty, fourteen; Duncan, that was left with Boyd, between ten and eleven; Daniel, seven; I, four and a half; and my brother, Alexander, two years and a half. She chose for her departure a moonlight night, that the people should not stop her; and so she got into Inverness about breakfast, having travelled nine miles. My sister carried the child on her back, Daniel carried the bundle, and I ran along side of both. In this manner we travelled from Inverness to Edinburgh, which is one hundred and fifty measured miles, in the space of two months.

Now you shall see the providence of God towards helpless orphans that are left to his care alone. As we travelled, we were the surprise of every one, as we were so young. Our money being expended, we were obliged to beg our bread. We were kindly used by some and harshly by others that were againſt the Prince. One kind woman equipped us with a little bag for oatmeal, for people that would not take us in would give us a handful of meal. She gave us a round wooden dish also, which my siſter put our pottage in when she met with good people that would let her bake it or bake cakes of oatmeal on their grid-iron. The chief of our food was pottage and milk, or cakes and milk ; and sometimes, if we met with good friends at a farmhouse, we got a bit of meat. If it rained, we waited at a farmhouse sometimes for two or three days. On the journey we had two things to recommend us, although begging from house to house : the things we had on were all plaid, and of the fineſt kind, for an extravagant father cares not what he buys. Our apparel looked like that of a gentleman's children, and we had a great share of beauty. Oftentimes where we came folks would say : " Poor dears ! they certainly are some gentleman's children." Others, " What if they are a gentleman's

6

baſtards ? " so, as God knows all things that are to
happen, if he takes one thing he gives another ; and
he has promised to take care of fatherless and
motherless children : for nothing can happen without
God's knowledge. We never marched when it rained,
if it had been two or three days ; and, on a fine sun-
shining day, we played on the road till near night,
when we continued to shuffle forward. If we could
not reach a house, my ſiſter would cover us with our
plaids, and cut the tops of brooms with her knife
to lay on and cover our plaids. In this manner we lay
at nights for weeks, and always set off in the morning.
When we had any brook to cross, or small river, my
ſiſter would carry over my young brother, then come
for me, and afterwards come back to take my brother's
hand. One time, as she was wading a river with
Alexander, when she came near the other side, the
water overpowered her and carried her and my brother
into a whirlpool, where they floated, till a man who
was digging potatoes at a little diſtance saw her
diſtress, and ran to her relief. He took her and the
boy out of the pool, and carried my brother and me
over also. He then took us to a farmhouse, where we
had victuals and drink, and our clothes dried ; and at
night we were put into a barn amongſt the straw. If
at any time we happened to be benighted, and could
not get quarters, we sometimes lay in an old house
without a roof or any house near it ; another time, if
the weather was fine, near the roadside, amongſt some
fine broom. One day, in the morning, before we got

up, a lunatic who was coming along heard us speak ; he
drew aside, and stood over us for some time ; he never
spoke but seemed amazed. He then ran away as if
he had been afraid, and we were very glad. My sister
next night was told that he was out of his mind for
love. A gentleman in the country gave him every
year a suit of clothes ; he went where he liked ; he
would work sometimes well, and, when the work was
over, they would take some method to affront him
that he might set off in a pet without asking for any
wages. This they did not consider as any act of
injustice ; for, if he got any money he would hide it
under a stone, and forget where he laid it ; so that the
money was lost to the public. One time he worked
with a farmer for the whole time of hay and harvest ;
when the season of his labours was over, the butcher
came one night with his cord, his knife, and steel, felt
his neck and loins, told the farmer he was fat enough,
and that he might be killed in the morning ; but
before morning he was gone many miles. He often
told afterwards how he had deceived the butcher.
Many things of this kind we met with, too tedious to
be mentioned. When we came near to Dundee, not
far from the town, on the side of a river, there was an
old castle where there was a blacksmith's shop. The
blacksmith's wife was as good a woman as ever lived ;
she put hay in one of the corners of the castle where the
rain did not come in, and there at night we lay. In
the day we went a-begging to Dundee, and at night
we came home. She let my sister dress our pottage

and bake cakes; so we ſtaid here three weeks, after which we set out again on our journey. When it was fine weather and we came to a rivulet, my siſter washed our second shirt and ſtockings, for we either had no more at firſt, or else she did not chuse to bring any more with her. When we came to a river where was a ferry-boat, we begged our passage over. Then we came to Perth, where we ſtayed a week or two. The letter from my father was now so worn, with fretting and chaffing, that it was scarce legible ; but a gentleman made shift to copy it for us afresh. From Perth we travelled to Kinghorn, where we ſtaid a few days till we could get our passage to Leith. A gentleman who was a passenger in the same boat with us, paid our fare. Before we left the boat the same gentleman made a collection for us. He raised half-a-crown. As we passed through Leith we went into an eating-house, and had plenty of bread, meat and broth, for five-pence. In those days a working-man could dine well for two-pence. After dinner, we set out for Edinburgh on a fine walk, a mile and a half in length.

Now, my readers, let me tell you, that for what I have wrote hitherto I have been obliged to my siſter ; for I was too young to remember it. As we were passing onward to Edinburgh by Leith Walk, a country-woman of ours spoke to us, and asked my siſter where we were going and from whence we came. My siſter told her. She answered that Prince Charles was gone from Edinburgh, and all his army with him. On hearing this, we sat down and cried; and the woman cried out of pity. Then she took us to Goolen's Inn. Mr Goolen and every one in the house was surprised and sorry to see us in such a situation. Mr Goolen gave us some victuals, and told my sister he would get us into the workhouse; for he was a very good man and beloved by everyone that knew him. My sister would not hear of the workhouse, nor of any confinement, but took us away immediately. We strayed down towards the bottom of the Canongate, staring at the signs, coaches, and fine horses. At the house below the Duke of Queensberry's, in the Canongate, a woman who stood at the door, seeing us strangers, and in the Highland dress, took us in, and asked us several questions concerning our situation; which we answered. She was a widow, and let lodgings; her husband, before he died was a master-chairman, of the name of Macdonald, born near the place where we were born. The woman let us sleep in a lumber garret on an old mattress, and gave us an old blanket or two. We had a shilling left from the collection made for us in the boat, with which we bought provisions. Next morning we set out again, and returned at night; and in this manner continued to live for some time. When we were tired of the town, then we went and begged our way in the country. Sometimes we lay in a barn, and at other times in a barn-yard. In such situations my sister would not let us cough, lest we should be heard; and we set off early in the morning for fear of being seen. In this manner we travelled round the country to Berwick, and to Morpeth in England. We now began to get a little money and old clothes, with other things left off by both boys and girls.

In the month of April, 1746, we returned to Edinburgh, by the Cheviot Hills and Coldſtream. We went to Mrs Macdonald's, as before, and she let us lie in the lumber-chamber as usual. Brother Daniel and I, when we got up one day in the morning, went out to play with the boys, and would not be kept under command by my siſter, who had the young child to take care of ; so that, in the day-time, we were seldom together. We went on in this manner for some time, till an unlucky accident happened, which separated us all. One day, as the Countess of Murray, who reisded in the Canongate, was returning from an airing with her coach-and-six, my siſter and the child on her back, crossing the ſtreet, were both run over by the carriage. My siſter and brother screaming for fear, and the people calling " Stop, ſtop ! ", made the Countess faint away. Kitty and Alexander were taken from under the horses, and, as God would have it, no bones were broken. They were both taken into the lady's house, and duly taken care of. When they recovered, the boy was put to nurse by Lady Murray ; and one Mr Vernon, an Englishman who had been butler to Lord Murray and by him placed in a good office in the Excise, took my siſter for a servant, and clothed her. Thus my siſter and Alexander were done for. As to Daniel and me, we both of us begged,

and played our time away; strolling round the
country, and stopping sometimes in the barnyards,
and at other times in a barn. In town we lay in the
stairs; for about Edinburgh, as in Paris and Madrid,
many large families live upon one staircase. They
shut their own door, but the street-door is always
open. There was an opinion at that time very
prevalent amongst us poor children, of whom, after
the Rebellion there were a great many, that the
doctors came at night to find poor children asleep, and
put sticking-plasters to their mouth, that they might
not call out, and then to take them away to be dissected;
and indeed I believe it very true, for what everyone
says must be true; and the poor Highlanders were
more despised at that time by the Scots in general,
of the other party, than the devils in hell. So when
we passed the night in a stair or at a door, one slept
and the other kept watch. In our rounds we went to
see our brother, sometimes, at nurse; and one time
to see my sister, but she wept so much, that Daniel,
having more sense than me, said, after we came away,
he would not go again because our being poor and
helpless hurt her so much. Another day we went
a-begging to Mr Campbell's, a master-carpenter's;
and who should come to the door but one of my
father's servants? The man, on seeing us, was
greatly affected, and a scene ensued, which took the
attention of many. But nothing touched our hearts;
we had no sorrow, nor the least uneasiness. One
morning we strolled within the gates of the city of

Edinburgh, to see the fine high houses, and were taken up by the soldiers of the City Guard; for none may beg within the walls of the city, and the soldiers have an allowance for every one they take up. Our names were given to the Captain of the Guard, and entered in a book. Young people that could not find protection were sent abroad in merchant-ships, in a situation little better than that of convicts, though not under the same disgrace. Those who were kept in the guard-house lived well, by the side of a good fire, with three rolls and three pints of beer a day. In this comfortable state we remained for three nights and two days, till the Council Chamber met. But when the guard soldiers found who we were, they were very sorry at what they had done; for they were mostly all Highlanders, and from our shire of Inverness. They asked us if we knew any person in town. My brother mentioned Mr Goolen, at the Livery-stables, at the head of the Canongate. This worthy man appeared for us at the Council Chamber before the Lord Provost, and gave him such information concerning us as induced him to set us at liberty. We went with Mr Goolen; and, as there was one of his houses, next door to his dwelling-house, empty, he let us lie at night in a closet on hay. When we had a mind to go to rest, we got both of us together into a cornsack. We went out in the daytime, as before, a-begging; but at night we had a whole house to ourselves like gentlemen. Now Daniel, being the oldest and about the size of Mr Goolen's son, his only child, he got his old clothes, and played with the boy, and went on errands, and there remained.

I was still left to my shifts, and went out, as usual, to beg and play, for about one year. Sometimes I was desired to get in the ride, and at other times to ride a horse to a brook, about a mile out of town ; in which employment I very much delighted. At night, when I came home, I lay down at the door of a warehouse, till my brother came to bed. He always brought me something to eat, and some halfpence for the next day. One morning, as we were getting up, a woman came into our empty house, where she saw a plaid that Mr Goolen had given to cover us. She asked if we took that out with us. We said : " No—never." She went away, and as usual we left the door on the latch. But she afterwards came and stole our plaid, which contained six yards. Soon after this the house was let. We then slept in the stable in the hay-stall.

About this time, one Mr Frazer, a master shoe-maker, took me to rock the cradle. I did not like the confinement of this. I pinched the child in the cradle and made it cry. I was turned off accordingly, which was the thing that I wanted. I was now taken into a gentleman's house to turn the spit. They gave me stinking veal for dinner—I put it behind the chest, and set off.

I went next to lead a blind fiddler, with whom I lived four months. He taught me to play on the bass.

He carried the one inftrument, and I the other on my back. One time we went to a wedding in the country, near Roslin Caftle. Thither he rode on his ass: I walked in the middle of the road, and the ass followed. We lived well all that day, and my mafter took thirty shillings. At night we both lay in the barn amongft some hay ; but we forgot the ass in the field. When the fiddler recollected this circumftance, he sent me for him ; and when I had brought the creature home, I tied him with his halter to the ftrong beer-cock. In the night the ass drew out the cock, and the beer was spilt. At daylight I saw the place all wet, and told my mafter what had happened. The fiddler beat me well with the ftrap of the fiddle-case ; so, as I had got two shillings at the wedding in my pocket, I left my mafter, the ass, and the fiddles, and ran as faft as I could into Edinburgh. I went next to a farmer's, near Corftorphin, about five miles from Edinburgh. I would not ftay in the farmer's two days : like Lot's wife I looked back to the city, whither I returned. I now began to live off Goolen's Lane, or Close, and found out Gibbs' Lane, a little below, about thirty yards diftance. Mr Gibbs kept hackney-coaches and chaises and twenty horses. I got some victuals and drink from the coachmen and poftilions for doing what they desired me, and I slept in the large tub in which they mixed the oats and corn for the horses. In this situation I continued for some time. When I left my brother, he was taken to sleep in Mr Goolen's house. I saw him every day. About this time one of the coachmen's sons died, and, as I was all tatters, he gave me his clothes, which fitted me to an hair. When a coachman went into the country with a family, to their country-house, I went in the boot and came home with them again. And, when I told them, on their asking, who I was, they often gave me six-pence or a shilling, which I spent immediately with the coachman and postilion. I liked this life with all my heart. In October, 1746, my brother Duncan, in the Highlands, hearing that we were about Edinburgh, that our father was killed in the battle of Culloden, which is within twenty miles of the place where he lived with Boyd; that everything belonging to the rebels was destroyed and their houses set on fire by the Duke of Cumberland, came to Edinburgh, dressed very genteelly, with two guineas in his pocket—one of which he had received from the Laird of Grant and the other from Mr. Boyd—for he never tasted of poverty as we did. When he saw us, he was amazed, and grieved to the heart, and thought bad worse. He stopped at Mr Goolen's with his brother, and paid what he called for. Mr Goolen asked him if he would be a mason. He said: "Yes." So in a week he sent him to Falkirk to his brother, a stonemason in great business and credit, with whom he was bound apprentice for seven years.

Between this time and the year fifty, I became a postilion to Mr Gibbs, who set his carpenter to make a bed-frame for me over the hay-stall, in one of the ftables, and gave me blankets, bedding, and sheets every month. Mr Gibbs was a man of great possessions. He had a whole lane of houses, the largeft coachyard in Great Britain, a garden and a gardener. He put me in livery, and looked upon me as his apprentice. I was fitted out with a green jacket with a red cape, a red waiftcoat, and a leather cap with the forepart lined with red morocco. Mr Gibbs was a gentleman, the son of a gentleman, and dressed as a gentleman, every day in his ruffles, which is uncommon for men over horses and carriages, and never drove a coach in his life. The coat-of-arms he had on his carriage was a hand in hand, within a double treasure of flowers : his motto, the Gibbs' Contraɛt. He married a gentleman's daughter. Her father was the Laird of Craig-Leith. When he was courting his miftress, I always drove him in the chaise to see the young lady, and then I lived well. In those days genteel families took a coach-and-six horses, as there was no chaise to be hired, but single chairs with two wheels, and the second horse was often fixed to the left side to draw it along : so, in returning to town, the coachman would make the poftilion drive the set of horses ; and I was poftilion while the coachman was inside. By this means I learned to drive, and soon became the road-poftilion myself ; in which ftation I enjoyed a very pleasant life. When we went into the country with gentlemen's families, to their seats, we had good living on the road ; and, when we arrived at our journey's end, moft commonly noblemen and gentlemen

17

made us ſtay a day or two to reſt our horses.
My maſter pitched on me to go into the country
because I was light. When I was put on the horse
I had a ſtrap about my waiſt, and faſtened to the
crupper of the saddle ; so that if the horse ſtumbled
I could not pitch over his head. The roads, in those
days, were very bad. Travelling, of course, was not so
easy as it is now. It was therefore thought to be a
matter of consequence to have drivers of light weight,
and I was the littleſt poſtilion in Scotland or any other
country. When I went the Falkirk way, I used to see
my brother Duncan, the mason. He was very happy
to see me. He came sometimes to see us in Edinburgh.
My maſter, after a short courtship, married Craig-
Leith's daughter ; he had fifteen hundred pounds
with her. Soon after their marriage, she gave a feaſt
in my maſter's own house to the blacksmiths, wheelers,
harness-makers, painters, coachmen and poſtilions, and
helpers, and all their wives and children. My maſter
and miſtress dined with them, and after dinner, spent
the evening abroad, leaving Mr Gibbs' niece to
conduct the entertainment at home, with plenty of
wine, rum, punch, and ale, and a fiddler. Every
Monday morning Mrs Gibbs gave the ſtablemen a
cold joint of meat, and the broken victuals of Sunday,
and ſtrong beer. Now everything was agreeable.
My siſter and two brothers were always in town. We
saw one another frequently and wanted for nothing.
All the others had education. I had none, but
learned wickedness.

The year 1750 was a remarkable era in my life. John Dalrymple, eldest brother of Sir Hugh Dalrymple of North Berwick, Bart., in East Lothian, at the death of Lord Bargeny succeeded to an estate of four thousand pounds per year, in right of his mother, a daughter of Lord Bargeny's eldest son ; though, as the estate came by a woman, the title was extinct. Mr Dalrymple now changed his name to Hamilton. After he had been for some years in possession of the estate, and returned from his travels, he married Lady Anne Wemys, daughter of the Earl of Wemys, in Fife ; by whom he had ten thousand pounds. There was one of the finest coaches made for Mr Hamilton, at Mr Hume's, coachmaker in Edinburgh, that was in Scotland. When it was ready, the coachman was sent for it to town, with the old coach to be left with Mr Hume. The coachman, in coming to town with the old coach, foundered one of the horses, by giving him cold water when he was hot. So the horse was unable to work, as the new coach was very heavy, more like a state-coach than one for the road, and carried also a large chest of plate. The coachman found that, in order to take the coach to the country-house, he must have four horses. He went to several stable-yards, but he could not get black horses to match his own. They were greys or bays, or not at home. But when he came to my master's, whose horses were all black, he hired three, which with his own made four. And, as one must go to bring the horses back, the coachman pitched on me, as I was

light, to ride back the sick horse. So we set out for
Bargeny House, ninety miles diſtant, which, in the
condition of the roads at that time, was three days
journey. At the town of Ayr, eighteen miles from
Bargeny, when the coachman at the inn, where we
ſtayed all night, got in company and was merry with
punch and chattering amongſt those around, he said
I took great care of the sick horse, which I certainly
did ; for I got off and walked up all the hills, and, by
this time, Jemmy, for that was his name, had got
better. And as I pleased the coachman very well, he
hired me to be postilion for two pounds a year, all my
clothes, and a third part of the vails. Next day we
arrived at Bargeny, in fine weather, near the end of
April. The coach was admired, as well as the plate.
I was taken into the parlour, to see if Lady Anne
liked her new poſtilion. I was admired in my livery
for my littleness, being only nine years of age. Lady
Anne told me to come back again, after I had taken
home the horses. After I had ſtayed two nights, and
got the money, I set off with the three horses. I rode
one and led the other, and the third followed after the
other two. I paid for the expenses of the horses, both
in going and coming back, after I had got the hire, and
took bills from each inn. I took the horses and money
safe home. It was the firſt time I had been
out so far by myself, so I got great applause. I forgot
my being hired, and thought no more of it for a month·
As I was coming back one day, with a chaise and horses
from the Queen's Ferry, I took up two gentlemen

to town. They gave me two shillings for the nine miles. It happened that my master saw the gentlemen come out of the chaise and give me two shillings. He knew the gentlemen, and asked how they did. They said they had an opportunity of his chaise very cheap—for two shillings ; so, in the afternoon, when my master came home and I had given him the hire to the Queen's Ferry, he asked me if I had any person back with me. I said " No ". " What did you do with the two shillings the gentlemen gave you ? " He searched my pocket, and found the money which I intended to spend at the public-house, for that was our custom, amongst the postilions. He took and strapped me well, and took all the money in my pocket. I went, on this, to my brother, and told him what had happened, and of my being hired into the country ; so, on Sunday morning, he set off with me out of town as far as Fountain Bridge. He desired me to go to Bargeny, gave me two shillings, and returned to Edinburgh.

Now, before I go farther, I shall give a set of men a character they deserve—I mean the hackney coach-men in Edinburgh, who differ from all men in Europe in their station. There is no stand of coaches in the street on a Sunday. The postilions and helpers do the work in the stables, and the coachmen dress like gentlemen and tradesmen, and go to church, where they have the first seat in the Canongate Church, for all the coach-yards are in the suburbs. No man may drive a coach on the street till he enters into their corporation and have the coachman's word and whistle. By the whistle they call one another out of any house. The coachmen dress always genteelly. The coaches and horses are like gentlemen's. There is only one stand for coaches, and that is in the High Street, one of the finest in Europe, near the Cross and the Royal Exchange, where all the noblemen and gentlemen meet between twelve and two, when the musical bells are playing. It is a hundred to one but any gentleman in town may be seen there at noon. If a coach is wanted on Sunday, it is sent for to the master, and goes out as a day-coach. There is no luggage admitted in a coach there. There was not a coachman in Edinburgh that had less than forty or fifty horses. If any nobleman or gentleman wants a coachman, they send for one of them, for they are men of good character, and I have known them refuse a nobleman's service. In general they are more respected than in other countries.

When I parted with my brother, I set off with my postilion-whip round my shoulders, and one shirt in a handkerchief, which was all I had. I ran along about six miles, when I met a helper that lived with my master. He asked where I was going. I would not tell him. He took hold of me to take me back— I roared and cried. He kept hold of me, thinking to get a present for taking me to my master. The people asked me if I belonged to that man. I said I did not ;

so they took me from him, and I ran fifteen miles to Livingston to dinner; then I ran to the Kirk of Shots, eleven miles, where I stayed all night. I set off in the morning for Hamilton, ten miles; then to Streven; and to New Mills at night, eighteen miles more. I went to all the inns where the coachmen put up. Next day I went to the city of Ayr, eighteen miles, to the inn where I was hired, and there stopped all night. The landlord went to Madame Duff's, Mr Hamilton's sister, the sheriff's lady, to know if they had any letters for Bargeny. I got a letter, and set off in the morning twenty miles. I got there at noon. The gardeners, being at work, and seeing me before I reached the house, told me that another postilion had been hired; Lady Anne not expecting me, as I was a whole month behind my time. I sat down on this, and cried my bellyful, for I was afraid to go back to my master. But the head gardener, Mr Macmorlin, took pity on me, and desired me to go with him down to the house and see what he could do for me. When I went into the servants' hall, I saw the boy that was hired to be postilion, a stout lad about sixteen years of age, whereas I was a little lad, not much turned of nine. I therefore thought little of myself and sat down and cried heartily. I then sent letters upstairs from Madam Duff; and Master Scot, the valet de chambre, told I was below. The company, consisting of Mr Hamilton, Lady Anne, and Lady Eleanor Wemys, her sister, Lord Ray, and Miss Ramsay, sent for me. I went up with my whip, shirt

and handkerchief—my all—round my shoulders. Mr
Hamilton asked me why I did not come sooner. I
said nothing, but cried; for I knew in my own
mind that if my master had not flogged me I should
never have come at all. They asked me if I should
like to go back to my master, but they perceived tears
in my eyes; so I was sent downstairs, and the coachman was sent for.—" John Bell, you enticed this boy
from his master, and you have hired another. How
are you to do in this ? "—" Sir, he did not come
according to his time; and that is not my fault."—
" If you can send this country-boy home, satisfy his
father, and I will pay you; for he knows nothing
about being a postilion; and as for the other he
knows nothing but riding postilion—so go down and
settle it among yourselves." Amongst the servants
there was a division : for me, Mr Macglashan the
butler, Alexander Campbell, Lady Anne's footman,
who afterwards kept the great Inn at Perth, and Mr
Macmorlin, the head-gardener ; all the rest, being
low-country people, were against me; but all the
ladies were for me. The other lad, therefore, was
sent away. He swore revenge against me whenever
he should meet me. Lady Anne now set the housekeeper to make shirts and stocks for me; and I had
new liveries, boots and shoes. In the course of that
summer and harvest the Bargeny family visited a great
deal; so I came into a pleasant life. Though I
remained longer at begging than my sister or brother,
I met the greatest pleasure at last. Bargeny is

situated in a fine valley, about twelve miles long, and three broad, with a river running through the middle called the Water of Girvan, which on each side receives brooks from the hills, which are well covered with woods and parks. Sir John Whiteford's house is the first; then the seat of Barskimming; next Sir Adam Ferguson's of Kilkerran; Colonel Kennedy's at Drumbart; Mr Kennedy's of Dol-wherren; Mr Macheath of Brunstoh; next Bargeny; Sir John Cathcart at Killochan; on one side Boyd of Pinkhills, and on the other side of the river Boyd of Tarchrig; and at the bottom of the river the town of Girven, which belongs to Bargeny. Near this, by the seaside, is the seat of Mr Crawford of Ardmillan; and just opposite to this valley, twenty-four miles in the sea, a very high hill called Ailsa, which contains solan-geese and many other birds. It belongs to the Earl of Cassillis. My master had a large estate of twenty thousand acres of ground. He loved to encourage all trades. He had salt-pans by the sea-side and several coal pits. He had shepherds in the mountains, thirty milch cows, eight young fellows for gardeners; he had also goats and asses, for milk and whey in the season. Mr Macmorlin, as already observed, was head-gardener; Mr Craig over the farmers; Mr Maccrinel over the parks and cattle; Mr Macconnel over the hedgers and ditchers; Mr Heaton over all the salt-pans; and Mr Whorter over all the milch-cows; Mr Davidson over the carpenters and coopers; and Mr MacMichin head-smith. He

soon raised his estate from four thousand to six
thousand pounds a year, by renewing the old leases,
besides his own fortune before he came to the estate
of Bargeny, and his lady's. The family have eight
upper or lady-maids, four chamber-maids, two
laundry-maids, two dairy-maids, a plain-worker, a
first and second man-cook, a kitchen-maid, a butler,
two footmen, a coachman, with postilions and helpers.
—Lady Polly and Lady Nelly Wemys were often there :
they had each of them about five hundred pounds per
year, and each a maid and footman. The oldest sister,
Lady Betty, was married to Sir James Stuart, who
joined Prince Charles in 1745, in company with his
wife's brother, Lord Elcho ; so that the attendance
on Mr Hamilton some mornings, of his farmers and
headmen, was like a little levee.

After the new coach was come, that summer and
harvest we rode all over the west of Scotland. One
fine day, as the family was going from the Earl of
Cassillis's to Ayr, and Lady Anne was looking out of the
coach to see the country, my postilion horse stumbled,
and I fell over his head. Lady Anne screamed, and
fainted away. The coachman stopped the six horses
before the wheels touched me ; and, as God would
have it, the horses stepped carefully over me, so that I
was not much hurt. I was now obliged to take to my
old way of having a strap round my waist, and fixed
to the crupper of the saddle.—Another day, as we
were going through an avenue down to the Earl of

Dumfries's, at Lochnores, my Laird, who happened to be looking out of the window, said to Lady Dumfries : " I see the coach and horses, with the coachman and two footmen riding after, but I can see no postilion." I was very small and wore a dark brown jacket, as my scarlet jacket was not come from Edinburgh.

When the family returned to Bargeny, I had a great desire to learn to read, and the servants gave me a lesson when time permitted. Wherever I went, I always took the spelling book with me. I thought that if once I could read the Bible, I should not go to hell. In the winter the whole family went to live in Ayr, where almost all the families came from their country-houses to spend the winter in routs and assemblies.

Next year the Bargeny family made a tour of all the east part of Scotland. We set off from Bargeny in the month of May for Edinburgh. I called to see my old master. Mr Gibbs, in place of being angry, was glad to see me dressed in a scarlet jacket, trimmed with silver ; and, as I had about a guinea, I treated my old friends the coachmen and postilions. I saw my sister and my young brother. My brother Daniel was on the point of binding himself to a plaisterer and stucco-worker at Haddington, for seven years. We visited about the Lothians a great while. At last we went to the Earl of Murray's. The Countess of Murray was a relation of Lady Anne's. The servants were telling in the hall that Lady Murray had a boy of my name at nurse that had been run down some years ago by the horses in the Canongate. I made answer that he was my brother, and that I had been to the nurse's to see him. I also took occasion to mention my sister, and all that had happened to our family. This account went into the parlour, and I was sent for by Lady Murray, who asked me if I knew Alexander Macdonald ? I answered I did, and that he was my brother. It was now whispered about what my father was ; and from that time I was more in favour than before ; for Lady Anne's brother, Lord Elcho, and her sister's husband, Sir James Stuart, had borne arms on the side of Prince Charles ; and the Earl of Murray's name was Stuart. We visited in the three Lothians, and Fifeshire, the Earl of Murray ; the Earl of Balcarris, my master's brother-in-law ; the Earl of Wemys, my lady's father ; at the Earl of Haddington's ; Lord Colston's ; Hamilton's of Puncaitland ; Sir Hugh Dalrymple's, my master's brother ; Mr Charteris, my lady's second brother, who changed his name for an estate of twenty thousand per year, the richest commoner in Scotland. The estate came by his mother the Countess of Wemys, being the only daughter of the infamous Charteris. The third son of the Earl of Wemys had his father's estate, because the eldest son, Lord Elcho, forfeited his right thereto. From East Lothian we set off for Dunce Wells in the shire of Berwick, a place of great resort for nobility in those years, situated in as fine

a country as any in Great Britain. In the morning
the company went to the Wells in their coaches, came
home to breakfaſt, before dinner went an airing, and
at night to ball. Another thing contributed to render
Dunce Wells very agreeable and pleasant. The noblemen and gentlemen that have eſtates by the Tweed
side, in the summer and harveſt give what they call
a kettle of fish. The entertainment is conducted in
the following manner. They all have marquées for
the purpose, which they pitch near the banks of the
river. Orders are given for a large dinner, and plenty
of wine and punch. The fishermen take the salmons
out of the water, and that moment cut them in pieces,
throw them into boiling water, and when done, serve
them up on table. This treat is called a " krab of
fish ". There is always music to play after dinner.
Some of the company walk along the banks of the
Tweed ; others play at cards ; and the younger part
of the gentlemen and ladies dance country-dances on
the grass. They conclude with tea and syllabubs ;
and then go home. It is the cuſtom for ſtrangers
too to give entertainments of this kind, as well
as gentlemen who reside in the neighbourhood.
There are often fifty or sixty in company besides
servants.

We went for one week to Leith Races, and returned
to the Wells, and remained till October. We went a
short time to Bargeny, and to Edinburgh all the
winter.

About this time Lady Anne's two sisters were married: Lady Nelly married Colonel Dalrymple, Lady Polly a French nobleman. In the spring of the year the family went from Edinburgh home. Lady Anne at this time had for companions Miss Duff, Mr Hamilton's niece, afterwards Countess of Dumfries; Sir John Cathcart's daughter, Miss Cathcart; Miss Ramsay from Ayr; and Miss Crawford of Ardmillan. All these young ladies, with the Miss Kennedys of Drumburle, came and accompanied Lady Anne in their turns, and went out with her in the coach till they married off by degrees.

When Mr Hamilton and Lady Anne were informed that I was desirous to learn to read, they put me to school, as there was not much to do, only when the coach-and-six was wanted or when any of those young ladies went home or a visiting; for then I was always sent with them, with two little ponies, because I was light. In the course of time I got reading, writing, and arithmetic; but the coachman became jealous, and gave me a flogging; for, when he was out with the coach-and-four horses, he thought I did not give all the vails I got when I gave gentlemen their horses. The helper, being a labourer and not in livery, was not allowed to lead a horse out. The coachman flogged me sometimes till the blood came out of my legs. At such times I went crying to Mr Hamilton. Then the coachman was called, to know what his flogging was for. He told Mr Hamilton that I neglected to clean the ftable, or harness, or coach or chariot. I had taken to keep foxes, hares, ravens, otters, magpies, and the eagle, etc., etc. He said I minded these things more than my business. This passed on for a great while, for Mr Hamilton did not know the right. As the cooks gave me raw meat for my birds and beafts, I assifted them in the kitchen, particularly in the evening, when I had nothing to do in the ftables. By this I learned a little of the art of cookery.

As my troubles drove me to be religious, and to read the Bible, the coachman damned me, and said, I difturbed the horses by praying. I never went to a fair, harveft, or any merrymaking. If any person died within a mile or two, I went and sat up with the dead; and there we all told ftories and talked on religious matters. I was always to be found at those wakes.

If the firft and second cook went out to dancing or any merrymaking, they always pitched upon me to ftay in the kitchen with the maid and dress supper. Then I made pancakes for myself, as many as I pleased. If any other person wanted to go out, they asked me to do for them, and I did.

The people in the weft of Scotland are very religious; and I, hearing of so many good people that had died and knew beforehand the exact time of their death

had the vanity to think that I should make my peace
with God and know when I should die. I have prayed
a hundred times that I might die, having heard so
much about heaven. I commonly, when supper was
carried up into the dining-room, went by myself into
a private part of the garden and kneeled down to
pray to God. I had a great desire to see the Devil ;
and often looked behind me to see if I could see him,
that I might rebuke him ; for I was confident he could
not hurt me.

I had nothing to do in the evening but be in the
kitchen or see the servants at diversion in the hall.
I often went out with the two greyhounds and brought
in a hare. That sport I much delighted in ; as also
going out with the tame otter to catch fish. As for
my fox, when he could break his chain he would go
out four or five miles in the night, kill the fowls in the
gentlemen's henhouses, and come home in the morning. But before he was three years old, he was killed
by some of the gentlemen's servants.

The coachman ſtill continued his severity to me ;
often flogging me unmercifully and turning me out of
the ſtables. The servants desired me to speak to
Mr Hamilton in the garden in the morning. Mr
Hamilton could not tell Lady Anne, for she gave me
shirts, ſtockings, and neckcloths, and ordered the
housekeeper to take care of me. My master did not
know what to do. He did not like to turn Bell away ;

for his family was there. When Mr Hamilton got a servant that answered his purpose, he desired him to bring his family; and he gave them houses, so that on each side of the road, a quarter of a mile from Bargeny there was a little village, with gardens behind the houses, enclosed with a ditch, and two rows of hedges; for which houses he made them pay a small rent yearly.

The coachman took another method to get the money from me; but I muſt firſt tell how I got it myself. We had two little ponies that seldom went out but when I went with them. I went twice a week for the letters to Maybole, the poſt-town; and I was often sent on a message to Ayr to Mr Duff's. And I was often going out with the young ladies, taking them home or going for them, or, at the holiday times, for Mr Duff's sons to ſtay a few weeks, when I used to ride out with them. By all this I got money; for in those days there was money in plenty, as trade flourished and there were not many taxes. When I came home, John Bell would ask me what I had got. I commonly denied that I had got any-thing; but he searched my pocket and told me he would take care of it; and that he would give me his daughter when we grew up, so that it would be all the same to me when I had her for a wife; and he desired me to mark it all down. After this, when I came home, I hid my money in holes, and some of it is there to this day; for it slipped down so that I could never get it out again.

In 1754 our family made a tour of the West Highlands. We set off in the beginning of May by Ayr,
Glasgow, and Dumbarton. We next went to Luss,
where my master stayed three weeks at Mr Leach's inns
and drank goat's-whey. Luss is a village close by the
side of Lock Lomond. This lake is freshwater,
twentyfour miles long, and across between Luss and
the Duke of Montrose's house eight miles. In other
parts the lake is not so broad. Sir James Colquhoun's
house is at the bottom of the lake. There are twenty-
four islands in it that belong to the Duke and Sir
James. Some of these are covered with fir, with
birds, and with deer. My master and lady went in
a boat at different times to see them all, and an airing
by the side of the lake, every day. On each side of the
lake are high mountains. We left Luss and went to
the Tarbet, ten miles further, on the side of the lake.
There we stayed all night, right over against the great
mountain of Ben Lomond, where the snow lay on the
north side almost the whole year ; and in the finest
day in summer a cloud covers it like an umbrella ;
and by the shape of the cloud they can tell what
weather it is to be. Next day we set out for Inverary,
where the Duke of Argyle's house stands. On the
road to this place we passed gentlemen's seats, went
over mountains, round great lakes and through glens.
Inverary is a neat little town on the side of Loch
Fine ; and the dukes place is at the end of the town—
one of the finest sights in Great Britain. The house,
gardens, woods, hills, and cascades would be a fine

treat for a Londoner. From this we went to the races at Leith, and returned to Bargeny in harvest, and stayed there the winter following. In the year 1755 the family received company at home. Then we went to balls in Ayr, and avisiting round the country.

In that year a report was spread of me concerning one of the fair sex. A pretty fair-haired girl of our parish was put apprentice to a mantua-maker in the post-town, Maybole, fourteen years old, about my own age. She came home on Saturday afternoon, and stayed with her mother, a widow, that kept a farm. She had to walk about five miles. The third Saturday after I saw her I spoke to her, and asked her if she would ride. She agreed; and ever after, when I came for the letters, she rode behind me. Even the two ponies knew her when they saw her, and drew near the bank for her to mount. Sometimes she came at night to meet me; and then I walked near home with her. So, in time the people began to speak of us at Bargeny, and made me much ashamed. One day Mr Scott, the clerk of the parish, came about business to my master; for Mr Hamilton was ruling elder of the parish, and this Mr Scott was schoolmaster where I went to learn. He had all the children in the parish, both high and low. He taught English, Latin and Greek. He kept an usher, and a woman for the girls. His income was greater than the parson's of the parish. He had a boy to teach those that were in the spelling-book. He taught his first scholars the shorthand writing. He wrote the sermon every Sunday in church, and taught the gentlemen's sons to do the same. When Mr Scott was not well on Sundays, the gravedigger gave out the psalms, and wrote the sermon as well as Mr Scott. Well, after dinner, in the second table room where Mr Scott dined, the upper servants told him of me and the girl; and, for their own diversion, called me in. "Jack", said Mr Scott, "I have been with Mr Hamilton about you. I hear strange accounts of you, about decoying away Sally Macrath. The church must be satisfied. I must have you before the minister, and all the elders". So they roasted me in this manner; and all the other servants were laughing one to another. It afforded them fine sport.

I have nothing to mention till our journey to Edinburgh. Mr Hamilton and Lady Anne made an appointment with their friends to spend the winter in that city, and to be there before Christmas. A house was taken; but, in the beginning of December, a great snow fell, which in hollow places filled up the roads. Mr Hamilton told my Lady that she could not go before the snow was melted, but she would not be disappointed; for she was very proud, and valued herself much on account of the great family she sprung from, Macduff that killed Macbeth, king of Scotland. She wrote a letter to Mr Macglashan, chairman, to send out her chair, with six of her men, to carry her through the snow. As Mr Macglashan, butler, and his wife, the housekeeper at Bargeny, were uncle and aunt to the chairman, he came to see them, and brought five of his chairmen, for he carried as one himself. After the men had rested two days, we set out for Edinburgh before Christmas, with the coach-and-six, the butler, first cook, and two footmen on horseback, and a horse in hand for my master; so when the roads were bad and deep with snow, Lady Anne took to her chair, Mr Hamilton rode along side of it, and the two ladies and lady's maid got up behind the servants. In this manner we travelled, and arrived in five days all well, in Edinburgh, where we continued till the month of April, 1756.

We stood at Boyd's livery-stables, at the head of the Canongate, six horses and two saddle-horses. The coachman had board-wages; Mr Boyd charged five shillings per week for me; but on account of the eight horses at livery, Mr Bell being so called, as he was a six-horse coachman, had his victuals for nothing all the winter. We both slept at Boyd's Inn, as well as boarded. Mrs Boyd had a brother's daughter that lived with her, and acted as barmaid, a beautiful girl of fifteen: she took a liking to me and I to her. I made her and the English cook-maid presents of ribbands, silk handkerchiefs, and silver sleeve-buttons, and Miss Cochran called me her sweetheart. The cook-maid made me often kiss her, and she liked me much. When John Bell saw how she liked me, he said : " Jack, you are a damned fool if you don't marry Kitty Cochran, for she will be a fortune for you, as she is heiress to Mr Boyd, who is rich, and has no children." He said : " Miss Cochran will you marry John Macdonald " : she answered : " I will." John Bell saw what would have been good ; but I had not the sense to see it myself. If I had seen it I might have had her ; for the parson that married those that came from England every week, lived within forty yards, and would have married us for half-a-crown ; but, if you will not when you may, when you will you shall have Nay.

We had a very agreeable winter, and, as God would have it, I had the best part of it. We never went out with Lady Anne, even an airing, with less than six horses, with the two footmen on horseback, with pistols and furniture complete. When any one of the young ladies went on horseback, I went with her. When Mr Hamilton rode an airing, I went with him also : the coachman was too heavy, and the footman had enough to do at home. The young gentlemen envied my life, and often said : " I wish I had as pleasant a life as you." If my master wanted to dine at a gentleman's house, he would say : " Jack, go to the inn with the horses, and there is half-a-crown to pay for the horses and you." Sometimes the servants asked me to dine where my master dined, and by that means I had it in my power to save a shilling or two ; and now and then Mr Hamilton would give me half-a-crown, which served me for pocket-money to spend in the evening at Boyd's. When there was company, the coachman and I waited at dinner, and I went to the house every morning for orders. When I heard that they were speaking of going to Bargeny, one day as I was riding out with my maſter, I gave him warning. He asked me for what I wanted to go. I said I was too big to ride poſtilion, and that I wanted to get a coachman's place. He told me, if I would ſtop, he would give me the saddle-horses and a ſtable for myself, and that I should be groom. I told him that would make John Bell worse againſt me than ever : I hoped his honour would let me go. " Well ", said he, " see if you can get a place before I go out of town." " Yes, sir ", I said. I am sure he had a great regard for me. God bless him to all eternity ! Next day he told John Bell, when he came to the ſtable, that he muſt hire a poſtilion if Jack should get a place, for he would not have a country-boy that did not know how to ride. I would have taken the groom's place ; it was as good as a guinea a week, but I did not like to be in opposition to the coachman, for I looked upon him as my benefaċtor, next to Mr Hamilton. He and Lady Anne were the means of my having education and being put in a way to get my bread. Next morning, when John Bell and I were in Mr Hume's yard, the coachmaker, where our coach ſtood, as we were cleaning the coach, Mr Hume came along. John Bell asked him if he knew of any place, for John Macdonald was about to leave Bargeny's service.

"Mr Bell, how long has he lived with you ? " "He has been poſtilion with us six years, since we hired him from your neighbour, Mr Gibbs." "Good God ", said he, " how old are you, Jack ? " " Sir ", said I, " I have entered into sixteen." " Well ", said Mr Hume, " that is a great charaƈter indeed, to live six years out of fifteen in the world in one place. I have received two letters for poſtilions, one from the Earl of Glencairn, for a set of horse poſtilions, the other from the Earl of Crauford, for one to drive the poſtchaises and four horses, to have the charge of the saddle-horses, and to have a boy to assiſt him, and to ride poſtilion."

I liked this place, as I was to have no servant over me ; and told Mr Hume that I had known Lady Crauford for years, when I was out with the ladies, as before-mentioned. She was often in their company, for her father had a house in the town of Ayr, where my maſter had one. She had been married to the Earl of Crauford at Chriſtmas. Mr Hume hired me for five pounds a year to the Earl of Crauford, the firſt Earl in Scotland, the chief of the Craufords and Lindsays. He wrote to Lord Crauford that he had hired a servant for his purpose from his neighbour Mr Hamilton of Bargeny, and that he would enter into his service on the fifteenth of May. Mr Hume let us see the poſtchaise that was finishing for Lord Crauford, one of the first that ever went out of the yard. I gave the man half-a-crown to drink, and was very well pleased with my engagement. John Bell hired a postilion from Boyd's livery-stables, from amongst the postchaise boys. Near the end of April we left Edinburgh for Bargeny, and I took leave of Miss Cochran. I wrote her a letter and she answered it; but absence is a great enemy to love; Ross, the waiter, got her with child and married her; so I lost her, and she lost herself. Ross was a good waiter but otherwise a bad character. When Mr and Mrs Boyd found they were married, they were both turned away. She bore a boy that was blind, and she herself broke her heart and died; so there was an end of one of the finest girls in Edinburgh.

Lady Anne never saw the postilion till the morning after we left Edinburgh, on our way to Bargeny, at Hamilton, when he was getting on behind the coach. As we were going away on the journey, Lady Anne asked what boy was behind the coach. Mr Hamilton told her it was the new postilion. " Is Jack going away then ? " " Yes, Lady Anne, he is hired to the Earl of Crauford : he told me he wanted to go, as John Bell and he could not agree." " It is very odd, after rearing him six years and giving him education, to let him go, and hire one in his place, and me never to hear anything of it." At night, when Lady Anne was going to bed, she said to her maid : " If I had known, I would have brought John Macdonald up to be my footman, and not to be used as he has been by John Bell."

We arrived at Bargeny, and, on the 13th of May, Mr Hamilton called me into his study to pay me off. He asked me what money I had. I told him twenty shillings. "Have you received any wages from me?" I said: "No, sir." My master said: "Jack, if I give you two pounds that will be enough for your pocket. Lord Crauford will give you money when you want; and I will give you a note of hand for your ten pounds, and five per cent. for it; and, when you see me in Ayr, call for me when the interest is due, and I will pay you." I told him I was very much obliged to his honour, and said: "God Almighty bless you; and thank you for your goodness." I got the note of hand, and set out next morning on one of my master's horses for Ayr, where I stayed all night; and next day I hired a horse, and went eighteen miles to Kilburnie, the seat of the Earl of Crauford.

When I arrived I sent the letter up, from Mr Hume, and, I myself being in livery, the servants did not know who I was till I was called upstairs, and told them that Mr Hamilton and Lady Anne desired their compliments to Lord and Lady Crauford. When I came down to the hall, the servants knew who I was, and came to look at me again, and said: "Pray, sir, is your name John Macdonald?" I said: "Yes." They said: "It is very odd, as my Lord has this day discharged his gardener, who lived here three years: he is gone to Edinburgh, and his name was John Macdonald—are you his son?" I said: "I never

heard of him before "; but the farmers called me his
son. Now Lady Crauford, till laſt Chriſtmas, was
Miss Hamilton of Bourtreehill, one of the moſt accomplished young ladies in Scotland, for appearance,
virtue and a fortune. Mr Hamilton of Bourtreehill
had four daughters ; Lady Crauford was the eldeſt ;
each of them had ten thousand pounds, but a fine
eſtate, at Mr Hamilton's death, was to come to Lady
Crauford's children ; and what money he had was to
be divided amongſt his daughters. Many gentlemen
of fortune in the shire of Ayr paid their addresses to
them, and amongſt them Colonel Montgomery,
brother to Lord Eglington, who wanted to have been
married to the eldeſt. Mr Hamilton offered him
ten thousand pounds ; but Colonel Montgomery
wanted fifteen thousand pounds down.

By this disagreement the match was broke off :
so, after this the Earl of Crauford paid his addresses
to Miss Hamilton, and she left her father's lodgings
in Edinburgh without leave or ceremony, and was
married to the Earl, by whom she had three sons
and two daughters. Next year Colonel Montgomery
raised a regiment of Highlanders on the eſtate of
Sir James Macdonald, his nephew, who was then at
school in England. The Colonel went to America
with his regiment for several years. At the death of
his brother, the Earl—who was shot by Mungo
Campbell, the exciseman—he got the eſtate and title,
and afterwards married Lady Jane Lindsay, Lady

Crauford's eldest daughter. If he lost the mother, he gained the daughter. I began the first night of my service with dancing. There were two fiddlers at Kilburnie for a week. I went begging to Mr Gibbs, crying to Bargeny, and dancing to Lord Crauford's. In a week our chaise was sent from Edinburgh, with the harness. We had four fine long-tailed greys, with good saddle-horses; our liveries were blue and scarlet trimmed with gold lace. We had a pleasant summer and harvest for visiting and seeing company. My Lady's sisters were commonly with her, or with their father at Bourtreehill. In a week after I came to Kilburnie, the groom's daughter, Amelia Burn, came to be chambermaid to Lady Crauford, under the lady's-maid; she was the handsomest girl in the parish or in the shire; her father, James Burn, lived twenty-eight years in the family; her mother had a house to live in, and so much a year, and took care of a natural son of my Lord's. James Burn died about two months before I came home, so I took his place and my own. From the first day Amelia took a liking to me, and I to her. Lady Crauford and the young ladies told her the imprudence of being so fond of Jack Macdonald, but all to no purpose. One day, as I was toying with the plain-worker, Amelia drove her away and struck me. I went into the stable, and said to myself: " If I toy with any other girl, it is all foolishness, for none is so beautiful as herself; and I must respect James Burns's daughter "; so I never put hands, while I stayed at Kilburnie, on any girl after. I called to see her mother every day. I commonly carried a pudding or some tarts for my Lord's son, so that it became a byword among the servants that the chambermaid and the old wheels became Jack Macdonald's perquisites. She made me shirts at her leisure hours, and I was as happy as a prince.

One day, as we were going to Mr Macdougal's of Castle Semple, as I was walking the carriage and four fine horses round the green, the two saddle-horses for the footmen and the side-saddle horse for my Lady's sister, following after the carriage, the young ladies remarked that they never saw any equipage turn out so clean as Jack Macdonald's did. Lady Crauford made answer : " I don't wonder that it is reported Jack Macdonald's father was a captain in the Prince's army, for he certainly is some gentleman's son, or some nobleman or gentleman's bastard." I might mention twenty things of this kind, but it would be the same thing over again.

In the harvest my Lady was brought to bed of her first child, afterwards Countess of Eglington. After she recovered, my Lord and Mr Hamilton, his father-in-law, went to see the Duke of Argyle, at Inverary in Argyleshire. As I had been there before with Mr Hamilton of Bargeny, I could the better describe the place to my Lord. When he saw the mountains, lakes, rivers and valleys near Inverary, he said there was not such a pleasant place in all Europe ; and he recommended it as such to my Lady, and told her that Archibald, Duke of Argyle, had invited her to Inverary in the summer, when he should come down from London; so accordingly they went.

The family of Crauford kept their Christmas with their friends, and lived at Kilburnie all the winter, for the last time. In the month of April, 1757, as I was going to the stable to my horses about five in the morning on a Sunday, as I looked back to the house I saw smoke coming through the roof very fast. I returned and alarmed the family. When I went into the house, Amelia Burn was just coming down; except her the whole family was in bed. None of the men-servants slept in the house: we all slept in an office adjoining. I told her to let my Lord know there was a fire in the house. She went up and gave the alarm; my Lord came down hastily to me. I told him the upper part of the house was on fire. My Lord and I got the key of the first garret, which was a place for all the lumber. We saw the fire was in the barrack room, where there were four beds for strange servants; but when there were no strangers the place was shut up. When we came to the door, the room was like an oven. I opened the door, and the flames burst out against me with such force that in two minutes it spread through all the other rooms. My Lord called Lady Crauford and her sisters, and took the young lady, her daughter, out of bed; and in twelve minutes the room where the child, the nurse, and the housekeeper lay, was in flames. They lay in a room in the three pair of stairs, at the further end of a long passage, which was soon stopped by the progress of the flames. My lady's sisters and all the maid-servants lay on the same floor; and, as there was no engine nor water, the noble house of Kilburnie the ancient seat of the Viscounts of Garnock, was burnt down to the ground.

A message was sent to Mr Hamilton, at Bourtree-hill; and the family went to the Rev. Malcolm Brown's house, the minister of the parish. Mr Hamilton came, and made my Lord an offer of Bourtreehill to live in, telling him that he himself would live at the house in Ayr. My Lord accepted the offer, and went to Bourtreehill and remained there. The servants' apartments at Kilburnie were altered for my Lord to live in when he came a shooting or to do business with his factor. Mrs Burn lived in the house with my Lord's son, and dressed what he wanted when he came. I was respected after the fire, for being the means, under God, of preserving three families.

In the month of May the family set out for Inverary, by Glasgow and Dumbarton; they stopped at Luss six weeks, to drink goat's-whey and take pleasure on and round Loch Lomond, and then went to the Duke of Argyle's, where they remained two days with the Duke at his palace. We went an airing to see his woods, hills and cascades, and a sailing on his salt and

fresh water lakes. We left Inverary, and went to
Edinburgh to be at Leith races. In the harvest we
went home to Bourtreehill; and soon after this my
Lady was brought to bed of a son, the Lord Viscount
of Garnock. In the winter my Lord went to London;
and my Lady frequently went out on horseback; but,
when her sister went with her, she went in the
carriage. She never once went out the whole time
I lived there, either on horseback or in the carriage,
but I was with her. If any person spoke against me
to my Lord or herself, she told me who the person
was, because I saved her daughter, Lady Jane, from
the flames. She delighted in riding out and coursing
a hare with the greyhounds. My Lord began to take
a dislike to me, for which I was very sorry—and, my
readers, I cannot tell you for what. Soon after this,
in the harvest of 1759, I gave my Lord warning, and
was discharged the fifteenth of November, being
the Term day, and Amelia came away with child at
the same time. I went to Kilburnie, and took a
room near her mother's, as she had a milch-cow and
plenty to give her. I gave her six guineas, and other
things necessary. I thought to marry her when I
got a place. I went to Bargeny to get my ten pounds
from Mr Hamilton. When I came to Bargeny,
Thomas Hardy, the English coachman, had been
drowned two weeks past: one dark night coming
from a public-house he fell into a coal-pit. Mr
Hamilton sent for a coachman to Edinburgh, and I
drove Lady Anne till he came.

About three weeks after this, when I got my money, I went and stayed a week at Kilburnie. One day I went to the minister's house and desired the favour of him that, when Amelia was brought to bed, he would be so good as to christen the child ; he promised he would and so he did. So one of my fellow-servants and I set out for Edinburgh, and Amelia went a little way with us. He asked her if she would like to have John Macdonald for a husband. She answered she would wait twenty years and then beg her bread with me for life.

When we arrived in Edinburgh, I lodged at my sister's house all the winter. She had been married some years. The young man who accompanied me to Edinburgh got a place, and I put myself to hair-dressing. When Mr Hamilton came to Edinburgh on his way to London, for he was in Parliament, he saw me, and asked me if I had got a place. I told him I had put myself to hair-dressing. " Then, Jack, call for me when I return from London." I said I would. I stuck close to the shop till May. I lost no time. I dressed the customers at home and abroad. When Mr Hamilton came from London, I called to see him. He desired me to dress his hair, and I pleased him very well. He told me that James Scott had taken the Haugh-hill farm, and was to leave him. When he went, he married the lady's-maid ; so Mr Hamilton hired me for his own servant. Mr Scott lived twelve years in his service, and saved six hundred pounds. Near the end of May, Mr Hamilton, Lady Anne, and Miss Duff, set out for Bargeny with the rest of the family. In the year 1750 I went with my postilion-whip round my shoulders; and now, in the year 1760, to the same house, to be Mr Hamilton's body servant.

I now set out on life, without conduct or this world's cunning. I was a greater plague to my master and benefactor than one would think. I did not know the value of good luck, nor of money. Coming into two such plentiful families, I thought the whole world was the garden of Eden. My master knew what was good for me; but I had not the sense to take his advice. Gentlemen know the world better than we. I was put out of my latitude by contrary winds—I mean women. Mr and Mrs Scott went to their farm. One Mrs Manderson took her place. She was not there three months till she was discharged and sent back to Edinburgh; and an elderly woman was sent for to be housekeeper.

The chambermaid spoke something about Mrs Manderson and me; and Lady Anne said I would ruin my soul with her. After this, a report was spread about the chambermaid and me; so the housekeeper always locked the rooms, as she thought thereby to keep us from meeting. As the general election was to come on next April, this harvest was spent by Mr Hamilton in the shire of Galloway, that he might pay his respects to the gentlemen. He took me, the postilion, and postchaise, and the helper, to take care of the horses. We travelled thus through the whole shire, making interest, giving balls and feasts to the gentlemen and ladies at Stranraer and Wigton. A pleasant time we had of it. We returned home, and in November went to Edinburgh, where Lady Anne lived all the winter ; but my master and I went post for London. When the Parliament broke up in March, 1761, my master and his brother, Sir Hugh Dalrymple, returned to secure their election. When they arrived in Edinburgh they had a mind to go immediately to the country. But the Duke of Douglas died, which stopped them for some time, to get all things ready for the grandest burying that had been in Great Britain for a hundred years past.

The procession took two days in going from Edinburgh to Douglas Castle. On this occasion there was the greatest feasting and drinking I ever saw. There were about three hundred persons, in carriages and on horseback, with all the family honours. All the company returned to Hamilton, and there dispersed. Mr Hamilton and Sir Hugh returned to Edinburgh, and directly set out for Bargeny.

My master set out for Galloway with the same servants as before. Our place of entertainment was at Wigton. The contest was great between the Earl of Galloway's son, the Hon. Keith Stuart and my master.

There was such riding back and forward, and drinking, for one month, that was enough to kill the devil. The election was gained by my master, who gave a ball to the ladies and gentlemen, and returned to Bargeny in triumph. I sent a letter to Amelia Burns and her son, to come to Bargeny. She came and lodged at the publichouse two weeks. She was much respected and the boy much admired. Six weeks after, my master went to Glasgow about business. Going through Kilburnie parish, he asked questions, and said: "Are these the walls of Lord Crauford's house?" "Yes, sir." "Who perceived it first?" "I did, sir; and alarmed the family, about five in the morning." "Have you not a child in this parish?" "Yes, sir, in that village before you." "Well, you may go and see him: I shall ride gently on." I went, and saw Amelia and the boy, and, having had something to drink, went after my master. It was only three miles to Mr Macdougal's, of Castle Semple, where he was to dine, and stay all night. When we came there, and my master had his shoes on and his curls let out, I had a horse from the groom, and went back to Amelia and stayed three or four hours. My master stayed next day, and I went back again.

We went next to Glasgow, and then to Edinburgh. Mr Hamilton returned to Ayr, where Lady Anne met him, and stayed three or four days with his sister, Mrs Duff. When they went home they took Mrs Innes with them, that had been on a visit to

Mr Duff's. She was a widow-lady, daughter to Sir Andrew Agnew, whose husband, when alive was very much in my master's interest in Stranraer. Mrs Innes wore a wig; and, for the head-ache, had her head shaved three times a week, without the least harm or evil thoughts on either side. But the lady's-maid told my Lady that I went into Mrs Innes's room very often before she came to breakfast. One night Lady Anne wrote her a card, and sent it into her bedroom, desiring her to make herself ready to return to Ayr in the morning, for at Bargeny she should not sleep another night. It quite surprised Mrs Innes, and she asked the chambermaid if she knew the reason of this card being sent to her. "Madam, I believe she thinks there is something between Jack Macdonald and you; for Lady Anne turned off the house-keeper, chambermaid, and her own god-daughter, when she thought there was any love between them and Jack. As you know, Madam, the Earl and Countess of Crauford have been parted almost a twelvemonth; and I dare say you have heard for what." "Very well, Betty, give my respects to Lady Anne, and I should wish to go off at six in the morning." The chaise was ready and she went to Ayr, to Mrs Duff's, to breakfast. Mrs Duff said: "What made you come away before breakfast, Mrs Innes?" She shewed her Lady Anne's card. "There is my warning for having John Macdonald to shave my head, the same as Jack ever does to me, when he comes to Mr Duff's." Mrs Duff was extremely uneasy, and said:

" For God's sake don't speak of it to Mr Duff. This is a fine return to me for Mr Innes's friendship to Mr Hamilton, at his election." My master asked for Mrs Innes at dinner. Lady Anne said she was gone to Ayr. " To Ayr," said he, " without taking leave ? " It made him a little uneasy for he thought that something was the matter. After dinner he asked Lady Anne's maid if she knew what Mrs Innes went away for in such a hurry. She answered : " I don't know, sir. Lady Anne sent her a card, but I did not know the contents." "Who carried it to Mrs Innes ? " She said the chamber-maid. " Send her to me." When she came, he asked her if she knew for what Mrs Innes went away. " Sir, I believe it was because John Macdonald went into her chamber to shave her head." He turned round and said nothing ; but it turned my master against me, as I soon discovered ; for next day a number of gentlemen met at Girvan to play at the golf or cricket. The gentlemen, after dinner, drank freely, and my master was in liquor. In the evening, when we came all home to Bargeny, he asked me for one of the clubs that was not in the chaise with the rest. I answered : " Sir, I suppose it is left at the inn." With that he took one of the clubs, and broke it in pieces over my back, and said : " You damned scoundrel—provide yourself with a place." Sir William Maxwell, Mr Kennedy, and Mr Macculloch saw him strike me. Lady Anne, Mrs Duff, Miss Duff, two Miss Kennedys, and Miss Crawford of Ardmillan, seeing my master a little confused, and I not waiting at supper, Lady Anne asked Mr Hamilton what was become of John Macdonald. But no answer. Sir William said: " I believe, my Lady, he is not come yet from Girvan." After supper, the ladies having heard what had passed, were very sorry ; but they believed me to be innocent, and so I really was. I was called up next morning to dress Mr Hamilton. Neither he nor I spoke a word about what had passed laſt night ; and I directly forgot all evil. We set off for Eaſt Lothian, to see his eſtate and his friends. On the journey he hired a servant of Colonel Dalrymple, a servant of experience, and Mr Hamilton made a man of him ; for in a few years he put him into one of the firſt inns of Ayr.

My maſter saw that I had no conduct, and did not know the value of a good place. When we returned to Bargeny some time after, there was a race of horses at Girvan. When Mr Hamilton came to Mr Stuart's inn, where all the gentlemen went to dine, he said to me as I was dressing his hair : " John, I think the beſt thing you could do would be to marry Jane Stuart, for by doing so you would soon make a fortune." " Sir, I am obliged to you for your advice " ; but I thought light of it, and thought no more of it. Jane Stuart's father and mother were dead, and she had the inn to herself. Next day, I told Mr Scott, whom I succeeded, what Mr Hamilton said concerning Jane Stuart. Mr Scott said he thought " if you was to marry Jane Stuart, he would have you then to go

with him always when he went into the shire of
Galloway ".

About the beginning of November we set out for
Edinburgh, on my master's way to London.   Lady
Anne accompanied my master in a coach to Hamilton.
There was one place of the road that was dangerous,
where the company commonly walked on foot.   My
master walked on, and Lady Anne's servants went to
carry her out of the dirty road into the footway.   She
would not let *them* do this office, but called me to
carry her.   When we came to New Mills, near the
Earl of Loudon's house, the inn where we stopped
belonged to the Earl of Loudon's head cook, whose
two daughters kept it.   He took no account of it
himself.   Half a year before this the mother had died,
and the two girls were left alone.   We knew one
another from children.   After dinner Mr Hamilton
called Jane Robe (her father's name was Robe) into
the other room, and spoke something to her.   About
half an hour after that, the woman cook called for
me into the garden, and told me she heard I was
going from Mr Hamilton's.   " Now ", said she, " as I
have known you a long time, if you will take my
advice, I will tell you how you may do yourself good
all your life."   " How ? " said I.   " By making love
to Miss Robe ; I am sure she will have you if you make
love in a respectful manner."   I had no desire ; but I
told her I would come back and make love in a few
days.   When I had left my master, I went in and called

the two Miss Robes to drink a glass of wine with me. That was the beſt chance I ever had in my life, if I had embraced it. We set off for Edinburgh the day that my maſter was to set out for London, to join the Parliament. My successor came to his place. Mr Hamilton told him to go and order a poſtchaise and saddle-horse, at John Bell's, his former coachman. "I shall go to Rock Vale, my house in Eaſt Lothian, and to Dunbar at night. If you have any business to do in town, come to Dunbar any time this evening. I shall take John Macdonald with me all day, and he can return with the chaise in the morning."

When I returned to Edinburgh in a day or two after, I went to live with Colonel Skeene, till the servant he had hired could come home. At this time I visited a person that had lived fellow-servant with me at Bargeny. He lived with Mrs Dalrymple, wife of Colonel Dalrymple, Governor of Guadaloupe. The French governess was turned away on my account, and afterwards the housekeeper. Then a report went through Edinburgh concerning me. Colonel Skeene told me of it when his servant came home, and desired me to go to London and get a place ; "for no family here", said the Colonel, "will hire you, for fear of their women". And the servants in Edinburgh said : "Damn you, Macdonald, I suppose when you was born you was thrown into a woman's shift, and that the women and you are ſtill ſtriving for it."

57

I went after the Earl of Aboyne's service. The Lady asked my name. They said if they wanted me they would send for me. I went next to a Mr Campbell, who, being newly married, refused me.

I have often heard the ladies say, as they were walking along the ftreets of Edinburgh, one to another : " Is that him ? " " Yes ", says another. I always went very clean, for I delighted in dress and powder. My name was commonly the French Macdonald. When I went into Mrs Bell's one day, I told her what I heard the ladies say in the ftreet. She said : " If you don't take care, the women will be your ruin." I said to her : " You have known me from the year 1750 ; pray tell me what you think ? What makes the women take to me so ? " " Johnny," said Mrs Bell, " there is nothing in it further than this—they think you have so good a temper, and never hear you say an ill word ; and you are so obliging in your way—for a disagreeable word will turn away the affections. But you are always praising their beauty. There was Duke Hamilton, that married Miss Gunning. He was very debauched in bad women's company ; but amongst ladies he was one of the politest and beft-behaved men in Great Britain. And there is nothing that gains the affections of women so soon as to be always obliging to them."

I thought I should never get a place ; but Montgomery, the hair-dresser, told me to go to

Major Joass, facing the Trone Church. "He wants a servant; make use of my name, as he spoke to me." I went to the Major in the morning. "Sir, I hear you want a servant." "Yes, I do." After several questions he hired me. He asked me who would give me a character. "Sir, I believe Mr Charles Dalrymple, brother to Mr Hamilton of Bargeny." "Very well, call on me to-morrow." When I came, the Major said: "I shall take you for my servant, for you must live with a single gentleman: no family will admit you into their house. I like a man that is given to women—that is gentleman-like—but to drink and swear is to be a blackguard." I entered my service next day to the best of masters.

At the house where we lodged there was a pretty girl called Kitty Hamilton. There was no other person in the house. Her mistress lived at another house, where gentlemen lodged. We breakfasted and drank tea in the afternoon together every day. She told me this gentleman and the other offered her one guinea; another two; another five. I said to her: "This reminds me of a circumstance where I was born. A young man loved a girl. He said: 'I should be glad to go to bed with you, my dear Jenny.' She said: 'You fool! Why do you ask such a thing?' I said: 'Kitty, in place of asking, he should have put her to bed without asking.' She said: 'That is the best way of doing.'" One day after, a chaise was ordered for the Major to go to Mr Abercrombie's of Tullibodie's; when he said: "John, call for me in the chaise, at Balfour's Coffee-house near the Cross, at such a time, for I shall sleep at Tullibodie's to-night." The house of Tullibodie was near Alloa, in the neighbourhood of Stirling, about thirty miles off.

When I was going, I said, "Kitty good bye", and gave her a kiss. At that time she was making the bed where I lay, in a room that had no light but from the passage. I said : "We shall be back in three days." I laid her on the bed, and began toying with her. She screamed out. At that instant a woman and two men were coming down the stairs. They all came in, and said : "Sir, are you going to ravish the young woman ?" I was very much afraid when they surrounded me and were going to take me into custody. The one said to the other : "Go and call the guard soldiers and take him"; but the woman said : "You had better not be in such haste; ask the young woman the particulars." "Pray, young woman, did this gentleman offer to affront you?" "No, sir, quite the reverse. I just received a letter from the country, of the death of my mother, which put me into fits ; and John only took hold of me that I should not hurt myself." "Very well, young woman, all is well ; and, sir, we beg you a thousand pardons, and will treat you with anything to drink." But I said : "No, gentlemen, I forgive, and shall treat you." I bought two bottles of old Port, and we drank them. I went after my master, the Major, in the chaise to

Tullibodie. One day, at dinner, one of the house-maids said : " Ever since the Major came here, our young ladies lock themselves in their rooms : is it for fear of the Major or his man ? " It went round the table as a joke. We returned to our lodgings in Edinburgh, and, after ſtaying a month, set off for London, in the year 1762, and remained till the beginning of June, when we set off for Cheſter, and then through Wales to Holyhead.

My maſter was much delighted with the country and the fine weather. The Major travelled very slowly, and every place we came to he had the harp played to him. At Holywell we ſtayed one day, at Connoway we ſtayed two, and by a contrary wind we were detained at Holyhead one week.

We set sail in the packet for Dublin, and landed at Dunlary, in company with several gentlemen. We all breakfaſted there. We hired two hackney coaches to bring the company to town, and a cart for the luggage. The gentlemen came out and went into the coaches, but the coachman of the firſt coach, where the Major was seated, was not in the way. My maſter said : " John, get on the box and drive on." I did so. By and by Dunnie Patrick got on the second coach, and they directed me which way to go for the four miles. When we drove through Dublin, along Essex Bridge, near the Hotel, the coach I drove broke down, and Dunnie Patrick came up in

such a fright!—but he saw it was not my fault. The
gentlemen crawled out of the upper window, and
said: "It is John's fault." Another, "Why did
John drive?" But the Major said: "Damn it,
how can it be John's fault? Don't you see the two
side-braces are broken?" Dunnie Patrick said:
"Upon my soul, I forgive all your honours; the two
side-braces upon the very one side are both broke, and
is it not a wonder now that the two braces on the other
side did not break first?—and the devil burn the
harness-maker, for they are both old and rotten."

We walked up to the hotel, and, as it was Sunday,
stayed all day. Next day we went to lodge in
Margaret Street, at a cabinet-maker's. The mistress
of the house was a Londoner. The master and
mistress were both civil, and I was very happy; for
my master dressed after breakfast: I seldom saw him
any more till night. He was amongst his old friends,
for he lived sixteen years in Ireland, in the Scotch
Royals, and in Colonel Bagshaw's regiment. He was
the best of masters. I very often walked about
Dublin, one of the pleasantest places in Europe.
The Major had very often tickets that he did not
make use of, so he gave them to me; and I, being out
of livery, could go to Smock Alley, the Royal Play-
house, the Garden, and Marlborough Green. When
it was wet I employed my time in reading books and
perusing maps, of which the Major had a great many.
He entrusted me to measure the distance of one place

from another by the scale. My master had always plenty of fine tea, of which I drank some in the afternoon, and with which I treated the maid, and the maid also at the next house, where a gentleman lived, who had a natural daughter. The maid brought her in to see the books and maps, with which she was much delighted. I asked her to drink tea ; and, as I behaved civilly and appeared genteel, she drank tea, and went out a-walking with me ; and to Smock Alley, and the Royal Playhouse. The two maids were very well pleased to see her go out with me.

Next day the Major went to lodge where he had lodged before, in a very pleasant situation, at the corner of Keppel Street. We could lie in our beds and see the people walk along Essex Bridge. Our landlord was a Mr Henderson, who kept a seed-shop. He was a Scotchman, and was very fond of me. I cut the children's hair. The mistress let the two little boys and the two little girls walk out with me. Mr Henderson told me he had a large seed-garden near Bloody Bridge, and that, if I chose, I might walk there with the children. As it amused me, I went with them. There was the greatest plenty that a garden could produce. It was all for seed. Nothing was sold or used but what he had in his own house. I brought nothing away in my pockets but cucumbers and onions.

It was always in the afternoon that we went; and, as I had the children in company, I went boldly to Margaret Street, to ask Miss Edgworth to go with us. She was glad of the opportunity, for she ate what fruit she pleased, and we brought her to her own door, which was on our way. When the Major dined in the country I went with him to many seats; the Earl of Rothes's, Mr Connoly's, and many other houses.

I thought myself in Paradise, there is such living; and the Irish servants are such hearty fellows! They looked upon me as one of their own country, being of the name of Macdonald, for that is a great name in Ireland. When my master and Mr Lowrie, Chaplain to the Royal Scots, and we two servants left Dublin, we travelled in two chaises, and our baggage went by sea. It is needless to mention any little village we stopped at. We stopped all night at Lusk, and next night at Duleek; and passed through as fine country as a man could wish to see. Duleek was out of the highroad, but my master wanted to take leave of his old friends, as he had been so long in Ireland, and did not expect to come back again.

Next day we crossed the Water of Boyne, and dined at Drogheda. Major Joass showed me where the battle was fought, and the stone where King William's royal standard was set up. At night we stopped at Dunleer, a pleasant town. Next night we stopped at Dundalk. Next day we passed by Newry mountains formerly famous for robbers. We stopped all night at the pleasant town of Newry, and next day at Banbridge. We dined next day at Hilsborough; as it was a fair day, and a great deal of merry-making, the Major ſtopped all night amongſt his friends. In the morning we set out for Belfaſt, where we ſtopped all night : one of the pleasanteſt towns in Ireland, at the head of the lake of Carrickfergus. Next day we went to Donaghadee ; from whence we were to take our passage for Scotland. We waited one day for the vessel. I went a-walking by the seaside to look at the beauty of the country. I said to myself : " What can be the reason that noblemen and gentlemen don't come to see the three kingdoms before they go on their travels, and become acquainted with their own country before they go abroad ? It would be of service to their education, and their future experience." We landed at Port Patrick, in the shire of Galway, after a passage of twenty-four hours. We break-faſted there, and went to dinner at the borough of Stranraer, where I had my freedom when living with Mr Hamilton, and where almoſt all the children knew me. In the afternoon we went along the sea-side, and across the hills, eighteen miles to the town of Ballantree, the whole of which belonged to Mr Hamilton. Next day we went to Girvan, fourteen miles diſtant, and dined at the inn belonging to Jane Stuart. After dinner as we were looking out of the window Dennis O'Flaghan, Mr Lowrie's servant, asked me ; " Pray, now, John, is this hill in the sea ?— is this now the very hill we left at Port Patrick ? "

"Yes," said I, "Dennis, this is the island of Ailsa."
"Devil take me", said Dennis, "but that hill has
travelled as fast as we have done for these two days."
What made him think so was, that the land came
partly round the island.

At night we stayed at Daily, a village near Bargeny,
where I formerly went to school. In the morning,
before breakfast, as we were preparing to go away,
Mr Charles Dalrymple, as he was riding to the mineral
waters near this place, saw the Major and me. He
was the gentleman that gave the Major my character.
He said: "Major, is it possible to see you here?"
"It is", said the Major. They breakfasted together, and Mr Dalrymple took the Major to dine
with him at Bargeny; so I saw the place once more
and the people; and Mr Hamilton ordered me a bowl
of punch after dinner. At night we arrived at Ayr at
Mr Duff's, for Mr Duff was a relation of the Major's.
From Ayr we set out for Stirling, through Glasgow,
about the end of August. The Major took the
command in the castle of Stirling; he had a fine
house in the castle, well furnished and plenty of
liquor. His aunt in Edinburgh hired two elderly
servants, a cook and a housekeeper. The Major made
one of the soldiers footman and groom, and employed another to clean knives and assist in the house;
so we began housekeeping. The gentlemen round
Stirling came to see the Major as he was coming to
settle amongst them, and asked him to come and see

them at their houses. The Major gave the gentlemen and ladies in Stirlingshire a ball and supper in the
town of Stirling. In the morning, when we came
home, he said : " John, which of the ladies took your
fancy ? " " Miss Fairly, sir." " I'll be damned but
that is the one I took notice of " ; and he laughed
heartily, for he was of that free and merry turn. I
never knew him angry in my life. Often, after he was
in bed, he would make me ſtand half an hour speaking
about things, after I had got the candle in my hand to
go out of the room. After this, Colonel Maſterton
gave another great ball. All we servants that waited
had a card hung at our bosom, for that is the cuſtom
in Scotland.

We went to Edinburgh sometimes for six weeks
together ; and at other times to gentlemen's houses.
A pleasant life we had. When he was going to
Edinburgh, oftentimes a gentleman would want to go
in the chaise with him, and offer to pay half-price ; but
he always determined to go sooner or later than the
time proposed. When he came home he would tell me
such a one was desirous of accompanying him ; but
he would not consent, as he was determined at all
times to be maſter of the carriage in which he travelled.
I always rode in the chaise with him.

When the Major had company in the Caſtle, after
breakfaſt was over and he was dressed, I usually put
on a waiſtcoat with sleeves, with a white apron, and

a cook's knife ſtuck before me. Thus equipped, I would go into the parlour to ask the Major what he would please to have for dinner. The dinner he wanted was ordered, and I appeared at dinner at the side-table. The gentlemen said : " Major, I never knew a servant like yours ; you muſt certainly give him great wages ". " That I do, indeed—I give him great wages." " What country is he of, Major ? " " He is one of the Macdonalds of Inverness-shire." The housekeeper was one of the beſt common cooks in Scotland, and she was up to the gossip in the parlour ; for the gentlemen thought I was the cook : she and I were upon very good terms ; and if she had now and then, a glass of good old Port, and some fine tea in the afternoon, all was well—and that we had. But every thing in time has an end ; for the Major was courting Miss Abercromby, of Tullibodie, whom he afterwards married. I told the Major : " Sir, I hear you are going to be married to Miss Abercromby, and, sir, servants that live with single gentlemen are not good family servants ; so, sir, if you please to get a servant by the fifteenth of May, and I shall go a little further ". He was sorry to take my warning ; but reason bore the sway : he was reconciled at laſt, and hired a servant in the country.

At the time appointed I was paid off, and came to Edinburgh. Near the end of May, 1763, I took my passage in a ship for London, and left all my friends behind me. When I had been a week in London, I met the Irish Chairman that carried Mr Hamilton and

Major Joass when in London. I said to him: " Do
you hear of any place for me ? " " By G——d,
Johnny, I do ; go to Major Libbelier ; he lodges at
a hair-dresser's in Lower Grosvenor Street ; go to
him, Johnny, early to-morrow morning." I went—
the maid told him I was below. " Call him up."
" Well, sir, what are your commands ? " " Were
you ever in Ireland ? " " Look to my recommen-
dations." He read them, and said : " I know Colonel
Skeene, and Major Joass in particular. Then you have
been through Ireland ? " " I have, sir." " Very
well, I'll give you fourteen shillings a week ; and, if
I go to Ireland, I'll give you sixpence more a day on
the road." " Sir, I agree." I dressed him, and he
was pleased. He called the maid, and said to her :
" You muſt make a bed for John, and I shall account
for it—and, John, you'll call me every morning at
seven o'clock, for I go out at nine." " Sir, do you
want anything more of me to-day ? " " No." I
came home at night, and said to the maid : " Shall I
sit up for the Major ? " She said : " There is no
occasion—he comes home before we go to bed, and all he
wants is to light his candle. He is a very sober
gentleman." So I served him two hours each day.
He paid me my money every week. About the end
of June we set out in a chaise for Cheſter, in our way
to Dublin. The Major hired horses through Wales
to Holyhead, and we soon had our passage for Dublin,
where I saw all my old friends. I had all the day to
myself, as in London. The Major was a polite man.

If he met me in the ſtreets of Dublin and I lifted my hat, he returned it ; but no more. One thing I can say, I never served him with a breakfaſt, dinner or supper, all the time I lived with him. When Major Libbelier was on the road, he sent me from his table what he left ; and of every bottle of wine he sent me a tumbler-glass full. Near the end of Auguſt he discharged me, having no further occasion for a servant after he returned from Dublin.

Next week I called at Mr Lamare's, in Holles Street, Cavendish Square, for Daniel Douglas, who lived fellow-servant with me at Bargeny. I told him I had left Major Libbelier : he said : " I wish you had been here yeſterday, for the basket-woman told us of a place. But," said he to the cook, "if Maſter John will wait a little, the woman will be here from the butcher's presently ". When she came, she told me to inquire for Major Deibbiege, at Mr Sandby's : he wanted a servant. I went, and was hired. He gave me a livery. He was juſt come out of Scotland, and had married a Scotch lady, Miss Seton, Sir Henry Seton's siſter. Soon after, my maſter made the tour of Norfolk, to see his relations. He went to New-market races, Swaffham races and Assembly, Raynham Hall, Holkham Hall, Houghton Hall, Norwich, Lynn, and many other places in the county. From the singularity of my livery they asked me if my maſter was not an ambassador. I told them he was an American scalp.

When we had seen all the places about Norfolk, we returned to London. I lived with the Major till after Christmas. He was not going to have a carriage; and, as I did not like a family so well, I gave warning.

In March, 1764, I heard of a place in Aldermanbury, and went after it. Two single gentlemen, Mr Ferguson, brother to Sir Adam Ferguson, and Mr Creighton lived together. Many others came after this place as well as me; but, as Mr Ferguson was born in the parish where I lived when I was at Bargeny, and by that had a little knowledge of me, I had the preference. I was hired for twenty guineas a year and two suits of clothes: they told me they did not want me to wear a livery. I went to their tailor, and was measured for one of fustian, to do my work in, and another of blue Yorkshire cloth; I did not want to be fine. I wanted to be like a servant. The gentlemen were pleased with what I ordered, when they saw them. As Mr Hamilton was in London he gave me a character. I entered home, liked my place, and was very capable of it. I was part of everything there. I marketed, kept the books, and had the keys of everything in the house. I was steward, valet, butler, housekeeper, head-cook and footman. I taught the maid to dress the Scotch dishes. When she wanted assistance, she had her sister, a married woman, to help her; and I paid her as a charwoman. We went on very well, and had always the Sunday to

71

ourselves. Mr Andrew Grant, of Broad Street, had a house at Hornsey. The two gentlemen went there on Saturday night and returned on Monday morning. When it was my Sunday to go out, the maid had her sister with her. We were very careful. We always had tea and sugar allowed us. When I was at home, I had sometimes one or another that came to see me. This went on near a year, and I was determined to take more care of myself than I had done, thinking on what was past; and I made a vow to this purpose. But no man can forsee what is to come. As I was going to bed, the maid's room and bed facing the stairs as I came up, she in bed and the candle burning, I could see her at different times uncovered. I went to bed once or twice, and took no notice. But one night the candle was very near the bed, and she nearly all uncovered: very tempting to a man, for she was a pretty young girl. I spoke to her, and told her the danger of leaving a candle burning, and falling asleep; so I put it out, and came away. From that time she could never bear to see me. A few weeks after, on a Saturday night, the gentlemen told me they were to sleep at Mr Bogle's in Love Lane, and that I should bring linen and dress them by eight in the morning, because they were to dine at Richmond. I got up at seven, which was rather soon to go to the gentlemen. I therefore took the key of the door, and went over to the public-house, to have something to drink. I had enough at home, but did not care a farthing for it, as there was no company.

Near eight I came home. The door was bolted. Susan went to bed again. She wanted to make me disappoint my masters. I knocked and alarmed the street till near eleven. I got in, but said nothing. I went to the gentlemen, and, as God would have it they were late up, and did not want to dress till after breakfast. When I came home the maid's sister was come, as it was my day to go out. I told her how Susan had served me in the morning. She was very sorry, as I was so good a friend to them. We had many words, and she struck me in the face. This so enraged me that I kicked her backside, and there was great confusion. I dressed myself and went out for the day. Next morning, she told Mr Ferguson what I had done; how I gave the wine in the kitchen to people; and that, when I made the Scotch soup, if it was not made use of, I warmed it up next day, if they dined at home and charged it again. My master told Mr Creighton; and, after they were dressed, I was called up into the office. My two masters were there, and the two clerks. Mr Ferguson said: "John, Susan tells me strange things of you, which I am sorry to hear; she says you struck her." "Yes, but she struck me first." "Call her in." I did. "Well, Susan, did John strike you?" "Yes, and if he stays in the house I will not." I said: "Sir, if you please, I will tell you all. On Saturday night, you told me to bring a change of linen to Mr Bogle's, and dress you both by eight in the morning. I got up at seven, took the key of the street door in my pocket,

and went to the public-house to have some drink.
When I came back, the door was bolted. I knocked
and walked there till eleven o'clock ; then Susan let
me in. I got the things and dressed you both.
Yesterday, when I came back from Mr Bogle's, I told
her sister how she had served me. She was so ashamed
that she struck me on the face ; which enraged me so
that I gave her two or three kicks on the backside."
" Susan, is this true ? " " Yes, sir, but he told my
sister lies of me." " Very well, Susan." But, my
master added : " She said you gave the wine away
in the kitchen." " Sir, certainly I have given a glass
of wine to Susan and her sister, and her sister's husband
and to several noblemen's and gentlemen's servants,
out of a decanter ; but oftener to her sister and brother
than any other ; therefore, sir, she is a wicked girl,
and ungrateful. Her brother-in-law is footman to a
gentleman." Mr Creighton, who was afterwards
sheriff of London, said : " As to giving a glass of wine
away, as you are a wine-merchant, Charles, I don't
think much of it." But Mr Ferguson said : " Here
is something worse than all that. She tells me, when
the soups are left untouched, you warm them up the
next day, and send them up to table. What did you
do that for ? to make me pay for it twice ?" " No,
sir, you are mistaken ; and if you turn me away and
hurt my character, I leave you to God and your own
conscience." He said : " Explain yourself." " Sir,
in cold weather, soup or barley-broth is just as good
the second day as the first. Oftentimes, sir, when you

were both dressed, you told me you both dined at home, but did not know of any company. Many times, however, you have brought home from 'Change two or three gentlemen to dinner. Then you would tell me to get more. You know, sir, I always had cold sirloin of beef, or haunch-bone, or buttock, and you had something of fish or of fowl. Now the soup that was made the day before saved us from the trouble of going for anything else. Sir, that is all the view I had in it, not to have to go out."

" Bring me your book," said my master, " and the butcher's bills, and I shall speak to you both by and by." They both examined the book and the bills, but could find nothing against me. We were called in again. Susan was told that they could find nothing concerning what she said of the soups—" So you may provide yourself with another place ; for, as you cannot agree any longer, it is best to part ". She went, and a cunning devil came after her. I believe the two were acquainted, for they met very often together. The new maid had a sweetheart, a porter in a shop, though she cared no more for him than for my old shoes. She asked me to give them a glass of wine, for she knew the other had wine often. But I would not. I told Colonel Roy's butler how Susan had served me. He said : " What can you do ? Never give a glass of wine to any person. If anyone comes to see you, treat them with a pot of porter or two, but always take care of your trust ; for, if you

do not, the firſt time you have words, they'll tell of
you." So I went by his advice. I had to teach her
to dress the Scotch dishes. One night I went to see
Mr Bogle's servants. The butler and footboy said:
"Mr John, the gentlemen were speaking about you
laſt night. Mr Ferguson said 'Mr Hamilton turned
away my poor John for fear of his wife.' Mr John,
did you live at Bargeny?" "Yes, I did." "Then
we underſtand; for Mr Hamilton and Lady Anne
are parted." "That is not my fault", said I. A
few nights after, Captain Hamilton was at supper with
Mr Ferguson, and the discourse turned about Lady
Anne. The Captain asked what was the reason.
"Was she blamed with taking up with any person?"
As I was going out of the room, my maſter said:
"With him firſt." "What, with your servant?"
"Yes." The Captain said: "Damn it, it is a
pity those things are ever known. Did he live
there?" "He was brought up in the family." I
was sorry to bear the blame, but innocent at the same
time.

Next our maid began her schemes. One night,
before bedtime, she was taken very ill, and, as I thought,
fainted away. I got her something to drink, and she
came to herself. She was so weak that she could not
walk to bed. I was obliged to carry her. When we
came there, she could not undress herself. I was
obliged to undress her, and to take off her ſtockings.
"Dear, how bad I am, Maſter John." "I am very

sorry for you, Ellie." "Pray put some water by my bedside before you lie down." I did, and went to bed. Another night she behaved in the same manner. I was proof againſt her; nor indeed did I underſtand her till afterwards, for I had not the craft of many. From this day she became my enemy. What a terrible thing is luſt! How terrible when disappointed!

One day the gentlemen dined at Mr Grant's in Broad Street. I went to the St. James's end of the town with Mr Duff's servant. We called at different houses and drank several liquors, which got the better of my head. Hugh Gibson came home with me, and bade me good night. I went down to the kitchen, and sat down in a chair. The heat of the fire made me sick. I puked, and fell asleep. Ellie shut the kitchen door, so that I could not hear the ſtreet door knock. She went to the next house, and sat with the maid. She expeƈted my maſter home in the evening to write; and so he did come, and knocked several times; but I did not hear him. Then she came to the door, and told my maſter she left me at home with Mr Duff's servant. She took Mr Ferguson to the kitchen to see me as I was faſt asleep. "Now, sir, you see how your wine lies on the hearth." He said nothing, but went up to the office. When I went to put him to bed, he said: "John, I see how you behave; a person I put so much confidence in, and to use me so!" "Sir, I beg your pardon; I went to the other end of the town, and drank different liquors, which got the better of me, and Mr Duff's man came home with me, and I fell asleep by the fire, and I became very sick." "Did you not get drunk at home?" "No, sir; I drank nothing at home but part of a pot of beer, when Hugh Gibson came home with me." "I can hardly believe you." "I do assure you, sir, it is true." My master went next day to Mr Duff's servant, to know the rights of it; and as I spoke so he found it. So this passed over.

Soon after there were ladies and gentlemen dined at our house. I gave Ellie a bottle of wine for herself. She drank some wine and porter, and by noon got drunk. The charwoman said: "Mrs Cook, the pot boils; will you skim the pot?" Ellie was going to wash her hands, and, having the soap in her hands, she lifted off the lid, and went to skim the pot. The soap fell in the pot. I took it out with the ladle. It was the Queen of Scots soup she was making. If it had been spoiled, I should have been blamed; and, if it was good, I should have had praise.

The Queen of Scots soup is made in manner following. Six chickens are cut in small pieces, with the heart, gizzard, and liver well washed, and then put into a stew-pan, and just covered with water and boiled till the chickens are enough. Season it with salt and cayenne pepper, and mince parsley with eight eggs yolks and whites beat up together. Stir round all together juſt as you are going to serve it up. Half a minute will boil the eggs.

By the time dinner was sent in, Ellie sat down in a chair, and, being overcome by the heat of the fire fell faſt asleep, and was as bad as I had been some time before. So ever after we never did agree. Now it was reported that Mr Ferguson was going to be married to Miss Fordyce, Mr Andrew Grant's Lady's siſter; and so he was, some time after. I went to Mr Grant's one day to see the servants. The house-keeper, Mrs Gordon, asked me if I did not live with the Earl of Crauford and Mr Hamilton of Bargeny. I said: "Yes." "Are they not both parted from their ladies ? " I said : "Yes." Little did I know what was brewing.

The maid began to dress away. Some mornings she would not have a shilling to buy sugar or tea, but would borrow from me. At night she would go out, and come home with gold and silver in her pocket. One day we had words, and I told her I did not think she got her money honeſtly. She went crying to Mr Creighton, and told him that I said she went out of nights along with him. He told Mr Ferguson. They were both very angry, and I got warning; but afterwards she lived with him, and had children by him. The firſt time I saw Mr Grant's footman he said : "John, I hear you are going away." "Yes ", said I, "on Ellie's account." "Not altogether for that, Maſter John ; the ladies say you are not a proper person to live where there are married people."

When my time was up, I was discharged ; and soon after I was hired to a gentleman in the city, juſt married, who knew my maſter. When I went for my answer, he told me he was sorry he could not take me, as a relation had recommended a servant to him, and he could not be off taking him. So I loſt that place, and was out of service till I had spent all my money, to the last five and threepence. At laſt a hairdresser sent me after a place, to be butler and dress hair, with a gentleman in Kent, and to wear a livery. The gentleman went after my charaĉter. I went for my answer. He said : " I went to inquire about you, and your maſter did not give you a very good charaĉter ; but I will take you by your looks." I went home, and liked my place well. I dressed my maſter and his lady. My maſter kept the best house in England ; he was a powder-merchant for the army. There were three more servants in livery. By the time I was half a year there, the housekeeper raised a report that I had taken up with the chambermaid in the country-house.

We jaunted round the country a good deal, in Essex, Kent and Hampshire. One day, in town, my miſtress desired the housekeeper to send me upſtairs, as she was going to send me out to buy something for her. I asked her what room my miſtress was in. She said the bed-chamber. I asked her if I was to go there. " Yes ", said she, " you are welcome enough there." I was much alarmed to hear her say so. If any of the maids said or spoke any thing that displeased my miſtress, she came and told me of it. One day, at the country-house, something was forgot for dinner. I took the blame on myself. My maſter spoke to my miſtress of it soon after, and she took the blame on herself. He said : " God damn you both ; am I to be disappointed in this manner between you both ? " Such expressions I was sorry to hear. I thought of what was paſt ; and I would rather have suffered death than to have been the cause of disturbance, for I had a great regard for my maſter and miſtress. So I gave warning to get out of it. One day, in the town-house, the cook-maid said : " Mr John, my miſtress does not know what to do, because you are going away ; she has not dressed herself these weeks." I was very sorry to hear all this ; it very much hurt my spirits, and I came away very heavy hearted.

Next I went to live with a Mr Campbell, for the time he was to be in London, to take care of his things and dress him. His brother, Mr Campbell, of Shawfield, lodged in the same house, and his footman was taken very ill. He desired his valet to ask me if I would go to the House of Commons behind his carriage, and to put on the livery greatcoat. I told him I would with all my heart. When my

maſter was dressed in the morning, and his things
put away, he wanted no more of me for the day. I
waited on them at breakfaſt, and very often at dinner.
I lived well. If they dined in the country, I went
with them. I was never happier in my own mind.
Before my maſter went away, he bought two horses,
and I got two guineas by that. I lived with Mr
Campbell till he left London. He went, in his way
to Scotland, by Oxford and Lancaſter, and made
several excursions, that he might learn the modes of
farming.

The week after his departure, I went after a place
in St James's Street, at a gentleman's juſt come from
Paris, one of the gayeſt young gentlemen and the
greateſt gambler that ever belonged to Scotland
(though he had often said he would never have a
Scotch servant, nor employ a Scotch tradesman):
John Crauford, Esq., of Errol. I met him in the
passage as he was going to his chair. I told him that I
heard he wanted a servant. "Who did you live with
laſt?" I told him. He agreed with me for fifteen
guineas a year, and half a guinea a week, and said:
"Come in the morning." He desired his valet to
give direċtions to Mr Bocquet the tailor, and he
measured me for two suits of clothes direċtly. When
I got the livery, he rang the bell for me, and gave me
twelve pairs of silk ſtockings in a parcel to wear;
and said: "I like my servants to go genteelly." A
few days after he asked my name. I told him

" John Macdonald." " What country ? " I said :
" From the Highlands of Scotland." " Very well."

It was now the summer. We lived in London, and
jaunted up and down the country till the winter ; and
then he remained in London. But, being poorly
in his health, he went to Bath in the spring of the year
for two months ; then came to London for some time ;
and then returned to Bath again. Doctor Turton
thought it most advisable for him to go to the German
Spa. At Bath he had words with his valet about the
bills. The valet said to my master : " You get worse
and worse." So he gave him warning. When he
came to London he parted with the Englishman, and
Lord Beauchamp recommended him an Italian, a very
good fellow, whose name was Henry. We set off
for Dover, and passed over to Calais. My master
took his own chaise with him, which I took care of, to
clean and grease. When we left Calais my master
asked me if I could make any broth, as I had boiled
him a chicken or a rabbit, with lemon sauce, when he
did not dine out in London. I told him eight or nine
different soups, which I described. But he preferred
the Queen of Scots soup, because, it being the month
of May, eggs, chickens and parsley were easy to be
had. So I commonly made him a little of the Queen's
soup, which he liked very well. We went post. At
the stage before we came to Lille we slept all night, and
went away in the morning, and forgot my master's
little trunk, with his money and papers. When we

had come three miles, my master asked me for the trunk. I said : " It must be left behind." He desired me to go back for it. But the French horse would not leave the chaise for me. I told my master that, if he would send the postilion back, I would drive the chaise and four horses to Lille ; which he did. I drove the four stallions the other ten miles. The postilion did not come up to us for an hour after we arrived in Lille. I drove so fast that the people in Lille were surprised to see an Englishman driving the King of France's post-horses. We went on ; and, when we arrived in Ghent, the people there were making ready for a grand jubilee, which had been preparing for half a year. The procession was to take place in three days. The Duchess of Northumberland was there, and many other English, and people from all nations in Europe, to see this grand sight. The Duchess and my master went to see all the preparations and all the churches, when ornamented. The beauty of the procession was beyond description, and a grand ball was given every night, with two bands of music ; so that it never stopped. We left Ghent ; and the next place we stopped at for a few days was Brussels, one of the finest cities in Europe. There were a great many English there. I went to see Prince Charles's stables, and his guards, and I was surprised to find how many English, Irish and Welsh were in his light horse, his guards. At Brussels there are the finest churches in the world. From this place we came to Liége, a fine large city. Here we remained all night, and next day set out for the Spa, about twenty-five miles distant. At the half-way house my master went into the parlour, and ordered dinner, and we servants remained in the kitchen. Soon after, a Dutch gentleman, his lady, and daughter, came to the inn. They went in with our master to dinner, and we sat at dinner in the kitchen with their Dutch footman, in a coarse livery and a large Dutch hat. He would not sit with us nor take off his hat, but cut some of the meat and put on his bread, and went into the parlour and eat it, and kept speaking to his master and the ladies, with his large hat on his head, about the roads, the postilions and the country. When his meat was done he came out for another slice, and then went in again. Henry and I laughed till we were like to split our sides, to think our master was dining with the footman; for Mr Crauford was so proud that he would not let a servant ride in the chaise with him, but would rather be at the expense of a horse. The gentleman in the parlour was in full-dress, in black silk clothes, and wore a dress hat under his arm. His lady was in a riding-dress; and the daughter, one of the finest young ladies I ever saw, in a riding-dress, most richly trimmed with silver. They seemed as much pleased with their footman's behaviour as if he had been a prince. We all set off for the German Spa, where we arrived in the evening. There was Prince Ferdinand there, and a great deal of company. The Duke of Roxburgh, Mr Smith, and our master kept house together at Spa for two months.

There is company at this place from all countries in Europe, in the season. No gentleman is allowed to wear a sword at Spa, by the Prince of Liége's orders, who sends part of his guards there, in the season, to preserve the peace. The company spend their time in drinking the water, riding out, walking on the walks, feasting with one another, playing at cards, in public balls, etc. A merry place, much like Bath in England, for the amusements.

When two months were over, my master set out for Aix-la-Chapelle, about thirty miles distant. We dined half way, at a large town called Veviers. Several plays were acting in the street, and many other sports were going on. My master walked out to see them. We left Veviers, and stopped at the next inn between that place and Aix-la-Chapelle all night. There was a great deal of company in the house, but the best room was not engaged. My master was let in there, he being an English gentleman, and supper was ordered. Half an hour after this, a Flemish lady and her maid arrived in a chaise. She begged to lodge there all night. She was told the rooms were all full. She said she would make any shift, if there was an empty bed. The landlady said they were all taken up where such a lady as she could sleep, but one, which was very good, in the closet of the English gentleman's room. " Then give Madame Blond's compliments to the English gentleman, and that I desire the favour he will let me sit in the room with him till bed-time." She was going from the Empress's dominions into France. He was very complaisant, and she came upstairs into the room with all the politeness in the world. She said she should be glad to sit in his room, as all the apartments were engaged. He said she was extremely welcome; and he desired me to dress some of the Queen of Scots soup, if I could get chickens, eggs and parsley. I said I could. As for Cayenne pepper, I always had it with me. They went to cards till supper was brought in. The lady liked the soup much. She asked if I was the Cousinier? My master said: "Yes." And I never lost the name of Cousinier till I came back to England; for I was mostly every day dressing one thing or other. After supper her maid and the housemaid made the bed in the closet ready. My master politely said to her: "Madam Blond, if you like, you may have this bed, as it will hold yourself and maid, and I will sleep in the closet." She said: "By no means; I am extremely obliged to you for the privilege of the little bed." "Come, Madam, we will play at cards for the large bed." They did so, and she lost. When the maid came to put her to bed, she gave her maid strict charge to bolt the closet-door. Madam Blond spoke to my master in French the whole evening. She bade him good night, and desired the maid again to be sure to bolt the door; for the bolt was in my master's room. Next day Madam Blond went to Spa, and Mr Crauford to Aix-la-Chapelle, where we remained one month, at the Hôtel of Madam Buches. The ballroom was in the same hotel. There was a ball three times a week. At dinner every day, there was company of all nations in Europe. My master jaunted all round Aix-la-Chapelle to different places; a pleasant country as can be, and the merrieſt on Sunday in the world. In the public-houses, dancing and fiddling; in the field, football and shooting at marks with bows and arrows. The shepherd-boys meet in the evenings together and play on the German flute, which makes it very agreeable as you ride along the road. When my master left Aix-la-Chapelle, he set off for Liége, in company with Count Odenonde, with his own saddle-horses and groom. John Pratt, whose brother lived with Earl Spencer, and Henry and I followed in the chaise. We were two nights at Liége. From this place we went to Brussels in the same manner, and remained there one week. My master sent home his groom and horses to England, and he went to Paris. At the next stage from Brussels there were only three horses at home in the room of four; for the chaise only two, there being so many passengers on the road. Henry had one to go on, and the poſt-maſter was obliged to drive my master himself, with the two horses. My master took me in the chaise with himself, though he never did such a thing before. I said nothing. But by and by he asked me some queſtions. Then I went on, and answered him in many things that he asked me. I was so well acquainted with Major Joass's History, and his Maps, and what inſtruction he gave me in them, that I entertained him a great deal. Next ſtage he ordered me a horse, for he thought it beneath him that I should ride in the chaise with him. I rode on two stages, and then he took me in again for another stage. He saw I did not intrude to speak till he began himself. What he asked me, I answered. He ordered me a horse again for two stages. Again I went in the chaise the whole way to Paris. I gave him an historical account of the families of Ireland, Scotland, and Wales, and a description of the country, which I was enabled to do from history and experience in travelling. I gave him an account of his own family for five hundred years back. I said : " Sir, it would be of great service to young gentlemen before they go abroad, to make the tour of Great Britain and Ireland, and there they would see the seats of heroes ; and learn many things, particularly among the people of Scotland, Ireland, and Wales, whose disposition is to respect former things, and learn their history without trouble. Sir, they are the most rural countries in the world, and the best supplied with fish and wild-fowl ; and they give you a view of mountains, lakes, vallies, hills, and rivers ; and to travel through those countries is the best thing a young gentleman can do to lay the foundation of experience, by knowing his own country before he goes abroad ; for the people of those three countries speak about religion, and respect the characters of great men. But here you will hear of nothing but eating and dress, and plays and operas. All wickedness is tolerated, and the Sunday is not regarded. The English often take up with

men's wives, and, when the same measure is returned
to them, they don't like it ; but in Italy and France
those things are not so much taken notice of." My
master said I would make a good Presbyterian parson.
In seven days we arrived in Paris, and put up at the
Hôtel de Parc Royal. We lodged on the same floor
with the Princess of Poniatousky and her sister, a
Countess. They both visited my master often. We
remained in Paris three months. My master had a
coachman, chariot, and a French footman. He did
not take me behind the carriage, but I got a French
master, the same as I had at the German Spa. I lost
no time to improve myself. My master gave me a
suit of French clothes, hardly to be known as a livery ;
so I became entirely the Frenchman. I dressed
with my silk bag every day, and still retained the name
of Cousinier, for I dressed one soup or other every
day ; and, if he dined out, if it was not far off I took
it to him.

One day he had the Duc de Lauzun, Count
Lauragay, Count Oudenard, Earl of March, Earl of
Carlisle, the Earl of Seaforth, Charles Fox, Esq.,
George Selwyn, Esq., the Princess, and her sister. My
master had always his dinner from the Hôtel de
Bourbon. But I dressed the Queen of Scots soup to
perfection ; it pleased the company so well, both
French and English, that my master next day gave me
two louis d'ors. I made different sorts of Scots soup ;
in place of barley, I put rice, and made it very strong

of the meat, well seasoned with herbs and cayenne pepper. I called it Soup d'Angleterre. I taught the Duc de Lauzun's cook to make it. The gentlemen made parties to Versailles, Chantilly, and St Cleod; and my master treated Mr Henry and me to all the playhouses and operas in Paris. I was commonly in the evening to wait in the way if my master should come home to tea. The Princess had a housemaid, a pretty Polish girl, to assist her waiting-maid. As she was obliged to be at home, I had her company often to drink tea with me, and to walk out when time would permit.

In the month of January, 1768, we set off for London. We stopped for some time at Almack's House in Pall Mall. My master afterwards took Sir James Gray's house in Clifford Street, who was going Ambassador to Spain. He now began house-keeping, hired a French cook, a housemaid, and kitchenmaid, and kept a great deal of the best company. My master and Henry had words, and the valet had warning to provide for himself. About this time Mr Sterne, the celebrated author, was taken ill at the silk-bag shop in Old Bond Street. He was sometimes called " Tristram Shandy ", and sometimes " Yorick "—a very great favourite of the gentlemen's. One day my master had company to dinner who were speaking about him; the Duke of Roxburgh, the Earl of March, the Earl of Ossory, the Duke of Grafton, Mr Garrick, Mr Hume, and a Mr James.

" John ", said my master, " go and inquire how Mr
Sterne is to-day." I went, returned, and said:
" I went to Mr Sterne's lodging ; the mistress opened
the door ; I inquired how he did. She told me to go
up to the nurse. I went into the room, and he was
just a-dying. I waited ten minutes ; but in five he
said : ' *Now it is come.*' He put up his hand as if to
stop a blow, and died in a minute." The gentlemen
were all very sorry, and lamented him very much.

When Henry was about going, my master had a
servant recommended to him by a particular friend.
When I saw him, and found he was hired to be the
valet, I was surprised that one who had no experience,
and was much inferior to myself, was preferred before
me. I was angry, and told my master so. He said :
" He is strongly recommended to me." So I gave
my master warning. What is to be must be. I
had farther to go than stop in London. My master
had now a footman recommended by Colonel
Campbell, of Argyle Street, one of the most accomplished servants in London ; he spoke French, and
could dress hair in perfection ; his name was Samuel
Cairncross, afterwards valet to Mr Seton, the Earl of
Panmure, and Earl of Dunmore. Had he been valet,
I would have kept my place. So I left Mr Crauford
with two Scotch servants, though, before I lived with
him, he said, he would never have a Scotch servant or
a Scotch tradesman. After this the people said that
I brought the Scots into favour.

EIGHTEENTH-CENTURY FOOTMAN

I went and lived with Mr La Motte, the hair-dresser, for four months, to bring my hand into hair-dressing again, for I was out of practice. One day William Boyd, servant to David Hume, Esq., met me and said : " I know of an excellent place for you ; as you dress hair so well, I know you will get the place. The gentleman I have in my eye has been in England five months, and he had a servant, a countryman of our's, who has behaved extremely ill. He is with my master almost every day, and he has been in the kingdom of Bengal these fourteen years. His name is Colonel Dow. He was at Mrs Elliot's yesterday, and I heard him ask her if she knew of a good servant ; ' for James,' said he, ' has used me very ill '." Mr Hume lodged at Mrs Elliot's in Brewer Street, Golden Square. " Go ", said Boyd, " to-morrow morning, and inquire for Colonel Dow, and tell him I sent you after his place." I attended in the morning, and went into the parlour. There was the Colonel and James Macpherson, Esq. They kept house to-gether. They asked me some questions. Mr Macpherson knew my former masters, so I was hired at seventeen guineas a year and a livery. The Colonel said : " You may dress me this morning, and stay till afternoon." After I had dressed his hair, he gave me two guineas, and said : " This is to buy tea for yourself. I give the maids the same. As for the boy, what we leave will do for him ; and I shall give you my old clothes, if you please me." There was in the Colonel's house the greatest plenty.

93

Things went on very well and I had many things given me.

The King of Denmark, about this time, gave his masquerade in the Opera House. I dressed the Colonel and Mr Macpherson as two Turks. The King and Queen were there that night in private. My master spent so much money on women that I was tired of waiting on them ; though, if many an hungry fellow had had in my place, they would have taken care of it, if there had been a thousand ladies. I gave warning merely on that account. My master hired a servant from Mr Adams, the architect, a Highlander.

The Colonel went after his character. Mr Adams gave him a good one. He said : " He is a clean, genteel, good honest servant ; but sometimes he will get in liquor, and he is given to women." " Damn him, I like him the better for that." " Well ", answered Mr Adams, " he will just answer your purpose."

Mr Macpherson, knowing me and whom I had lived with, recommended me to the Honourable Keith Stewart, brother to the Earl of Galloway, who sent his valet to find me out. He had taken a house in Piccadilly, and was going to set up a carriage. He wanted a servant in livery to dress him, and go out with a *vis-à-vis*. I went to him, and was hired ; and as soon as the Colonel's servant came home, I went to Mr Stewart. We had a fine *vis-à-vis*, and as fine horses as any in town. Our livery was the genteeleſt in London, richly trimmed with silver and the coachman and grooms turned out as clean as any servants in London. Mr Stewart was as good a maſter as any in London. If a servant was in fault, when he told him of it, it was only told as advice. He was a great hunter and a great gambler, and as accomplished as any gentleman in Europe. He spoke Latin, Italian, and French. He belonged to Pinksley Hunt. We were there very often, and in Northampton, and at Mr Knightley's, at Foasley. The Earl of Galloway and Mr Knightley were married to two siſters, Sir James Dashwood's daughters. It was the pleasanteſt life in the world to live with him. He never was long in London at one time, but from one hunt to another. There was not a servant in a hundred that could have endured the fatigue of his service. His hours of coming home were from two to seven in the morning. I have had the chaise at the door many a time by six in the morning, to go to a hunt, before he had come home. When he came at laſt, he would go upſtairs, take off his bag, change his dress-clothes, and go into the chaise. Wherever the hunt was he went, sometimes fourscore miles. Sometimes I have come seventy or eighty miles by myself in the chaise to London, and my maſter with another gentleman in his chaise. We went to Oxfordshire, to Blenheim, to Lord Foley's, Lord Thanet's, Stow-in-the-Hole, Cheltenham in Glouceſtershire, Hampshire and Bedfordshire.

The servant that Colonel Dow had got drunk often. When the gentlemen came home late at night, he would get up to fight them. The Colonel found he would not answer his purpose, for he himself was appointed by the Company to the East Indies. He one day called in Brewer Street to see Mr Hume. Mrs Elliot said: "Colonel, I hear you are going to the East Indies again." "Yes, but I have got a damned foolish fellow for a servant; he gets drunk, quarrels with the hackney-coachmen and chairmen, and knocks them down; they get a warrant for him, and I am obliged to be bail for him. I wish I had the servant I had last, Jack Macdonald, to go with me." Mrs Elliot said: "He lives with Mr Stewart—you cannot have him at this time." I went to see William Boyd, Mr Hume's servant. He said he was sorry I left Colonel Dow, and that the Colonel wanted to see me. I went and hired myself for forty guineas a year, to go with the Colonel to India. I gave Mr Stewart warning, and told him I would not leave him upon any account but to go to India. "Who are you going with?" "Sir, I am going with Colonel Dow." Mr Crauford gave me a character; my master did not know the Colonel. And I said: "Sir, I hope you'll excuse me, as I have a great desire to go away." "What the devil, do you want to go away? I used you better than ever I did any other servant. I let you ride in the chaise with me, and that is more than ever I did to *Carpeneto*, though he was out of livery; and if you were to stay, I would soon put you out of livery." I made no answer. He threw down his pen, with which he was writing a letter, on the floor, and went out. Gimcrack won that day, and on Wednesday, in the evening, Sir Charles Bunbury sold him for six hundred guineas. The Duke and Duchess of Kingston made their grand appearance there after marriage, after the Duke had had her in keeping twenty years. My master would not have been sorry if the Colonel had gone without me; for, when the races were over, he went to Mr Knightley's, and afterwards to Farmingwood's, a seat of the Earl of Spencer's, both in Northamptonshire. At that time there were nine or ten gentlemen and noblemen. Now you will see how God orders things that are to be. Lady Spencer was taken ill; an express was sent to Farmingwood's, and arrived at six in the morning, when my Lord and the company were at breakfast, before going a-hunting. Orders were given directly for all the chaises to be got ready with speed. We arrived in London in the evening. I went to the Colonel. "Well, John, you are just come in time to set off in the morning." I told my master at night that I was to go in the morning, as the ship was to sail next day. He had company at breakfast, and I could not get him to take the things off my hands. The Colonel sent the chairman for me twice. At last the Colonel's servant came; so I came away without my wages or board-wages.

When I came to Lisle Street, the chaise and four horses were at the door, and all the things ready to go, and my trunk in the passage. The Colonel, coming down ſtairs to go into the chaise, on seeing me, went into the parlour till I got my trunk on. At eleven o'clock the Colonel and I went into the chaise, and at night we arrived at Deal. We were put in a room with two beds. I brought the things into the room. Supper was brought up. The waiter said to the Colonel: " Your servant muſt sleep in this room, sir, for there is no other bed." He said: " Very well. As it is late, waiter, bring some ale, and a bottle of wine, and you need not wait." So I eat my supper in the same room ; and in the morning Captain Smith made a signal for all the passengers to come on board the *Lord Camden*, in the Downs ; and that day we dined in the ship, on our way to Portsmouth. After ſtaying two days at Portsmouth, and the ship had got her dispatches from the India House, Captain Smith of the *Lord Camden*, and Captain Savage of the *Duke of Cumberland*, set sail together : as Captain Smith was the older captain, he took the name of Commodore, and the other ships had their signals from the *Lord Camden*.

After we were out in the Channel there arose such a ſtorm that we thought we should have been all loſt together ; and we put about, glad to get into Portsmouth again with our lives ; and there we remained ten days. The gentlemen were at the Fountain tavern all the time ; we had nothing to do but walk about the country. At laſt the wind came about, and we made sail on the tenth of April, 1769 ; we went on very well, and the ships in sight of each other almoſt every day.

The firſt place we ſtopped at was Madeira. It was a fine place ; but we ſtopped there but one day to take in wines ; and set sail again. The Purser died on the passage. Sometimes one died, and the burying was always before breakfaſt. At other times a man or boy would fall overboard and bury himself. A lieutenant going out passenger to India, wanted to do the same ; but was caught hold of by the legs, and ſtopped from that rash aċtion, and taken care of. Something troubled his mind.

The passage is a pleasant life for those that have not much to do : to see the men catching the fish and birds with a hook and bait ; another ſtriking the fish with a gauge ; another time drawing in a long shark ; and whoever brings in a fine dolphin to the Captain receives a couple of bottles of liquor. We had a calm sometimes for a week, and could not get on two leagues ; then a wind would spring up and blow the one ship on and not come near the other for an hour or two.

The Colonel, on his passage, was writing the history of Hinduſtan ; and Mr Wood, a cadet, whom the Colonel took a liking to on the passage, he made him copy off what he wrote ; and he gave me the rules of the army to write from, in order to keep my hand in use ; so we three wrote in the Colonel's cabin ; and, when we were dry, I made grog out of his case ; and, when we were tired, we went to walk on deck : there was something always to be seen there—some of the men frighting or drawing a fish out of the water ; the porpoises or dolphins playing, or the smaller flying-fish flying over the waves from the larger ones. In the evening, all that could sing a song sat down on the gangway and sang ; and the gentlemen walked about and heard us ; and, in fine weather, the gentlemen visited from one ship to another in their turn. It was a pleasant sight to see the Commodore's boat let down alongside, and the gentlemen going to dine out at sea ; and, when they came back, the Commodore would sail about the ship like people walking in a garden, and we all looking out over the ship to see the gentlemen, more than a thousand miles from land. The Commodore called for the great iron pot they had for the purpose, and bound a rope to the two ears of it, and let it down twenty fathoms ; and then held the rope fast, to see which way the boat went, back or on our way where we were bound. The tide would carry us backward or forward, sometimes six miles, frequently without wind. When we were going to cross the line, just under the sun, everyone that had not been there before was to pay half a crown towards grog, for the ship's men to drink ; but there were three who would not pay—a Scotchman, a Welshman, and a Portuguese soldier. It is the custom to let those who refuse to pay down from the yard-arm, by a rope round their middle, four or five fathoms in the sea, three times each, one after the other. It was pastime to the ship's company. Each of the three got two bottles of liquor from the gentlemen to make merry.

We made the Brazils, in South America; but Commodore Smith would not go on shore. The wind, being foul, ran us to forty degrees south latitude, and then we were obliged to run back to the Cape of Good Hope to get sounding. After our departure we had a fresh gale from the Cape for Joanna; but a storm arose, which made us lose the *Duke of Cumberland* for a fortnight. We sailed down between Africa to Madagascar, eight hundred miles. By this time a great many of the men had got the scurvy by living on salt provisions; and two duels were to be fought at Joanna by the cadets.

We lost sight of Madagascar, and got sight of Joanna (a fine island and a beautiful view) in the month of August; everything green, the very hills and mountains covered with shrubs. We were greatly surprised, when we came near the town and anchoring-place of Joanna, to see the *Duke of Cumberland* safe at anchor. We came to, and dropped anchor; and the ships saluted each other with their guns, which made the hills resound.

The town stands on a level piece of ground, surrounded by many sorts of trees, in particular coconuts, with high mountains; and a large brook on each side of the town. The black people came on board from their canoes, in dozens, to sell and buy things. The boats were sent on shore for milk, fine water, and fowl; and the Prince sent word that he would come in the morning. That night we had plenty of milk and cocoa. The firſt thing that was done in the morning was to send the men on shore that had the scurvy, to put them into the earth up to the neck, and to remain there one day—which is the moſt speedy cure in a hot country. Their skin will be as black as coal, when put in; and in two days they were as well as ever.

At breakfaſt the Prince came on board to take orders: he was the King's son-in-law, a very handsome man, in the Mohametan dress—he did business for the King and himself. He was over the King's cattle; he was glad to see the Commodore; he had known him many years. He came into the cuddy, with the gentlemen, to breakfaſt; he ate bread and butter, with a little sugar over it. The Steward made him sherbet to drink; he took orders for bullocks, fowls, goats, and vegetables. There are no sheep, horses, nor ducks on the island, though it is thirty miles long. Each ship had a marquee pitched on shore for the Commanders to dine in with their company. Next day the Prince came on board; the Colonel took him to his cabin, and showed him books in the Moorish language, moſt richly bound in London, and piᴄtures of all the gods in the Eaſt. The Prince was aſtonished

to see such things come from England. He spoke the
Moorish language to the Prince, and made him a
present of some fine books of his own religion. The
Colonel asked him how many wives he had. He said
four, and that one of them was the King's daughter.
The servant that attended the Prince wore a sword
by his side. The Prince invited the Colonel to come
and see him next day at the house where he did
business, not where his family lived. He promised he
would next day, after he was dressed, and Mr Wood
with him. He said : " John, dress yourself, and come
ashore with me, and take a bottle of rum in your hand."
We went, and walked all round the town : at laſt the
Prince met him, and took him home ; where we all
went. The Prince made lemonade, and I put rum
to it, which made good punch ; we were all in the
same company, but I next the door. The Colonel
was a good man, and had the spirit of an emperor.
The Prince's three sons came to pay their respeċts
to the Colonel—fine young boys ; he spoke to them
in Moorish ; at laſt the Prince and his sons went away ;
and soon after the Prince sent a fine dish of chickens,
curried and boiled ; rice broth in wooden platters ;
and three wooden spoons and wooden plates. We
ate heartily, for it was very good ; and the Colonel
was very merry. He knew their ways ; but to Mr
Wood and me, it seemed ſtrange to see such things.
The slave-boy ſtood and wondered at us. When we
were done he carried everything away in a moment.
There was neither table nor chair, but sitting on a

mat, such as you kneel on at churches in England or lean your elbow on. The Princes came in soon, and made more sherbet, and I put more rum to complete it. He made a little for himself; for, on account of their religion, they cannot eat nor drink with a Christian. The Prince went out; and, soon after, came two fine black girls, the Prince's slaves, dressed in the Moorish manner; they had rings on their fingers, ears and toes, and bangles on their arms; their breasts were covered with various ornaments; a large ring of silver hung loose round the small of the leg: it was very light and hollow. They had neither shift nor stockings, but a thin silk gauze for a petticoat, and another, the reverse, from the waist upwards, fastened on the left shoulder, like the dress of a Scotch Highlander. The petticoat is full, and comes down as far as the ring on their leg. The finest dressed one entered first; put her two hands to her forehead, then to her breasts, and with her two hands touched the Colonel's foot: this is called a grand salam. In like manner the other paid her compliments to Mr Wood.

After the common compliments were over, I was going. My Master said: "John, if I don't come on board to-night I shall in the morning." I walked along the shore, and went out with the last boat, about half a mile by sea to the ship. At the bottom of the sea, round Joanna, the coral grows up like short spikes, that help the children in England to cut their teeth. The Prince sent the books to the King's house. In

two days he and his son came on board the two ships
with their attendants, and a band of music like two or
three old bagpipes, such as they take through the ſtreets
of London with the dancing-bears. The King was a
ſtout old man, his own son a genteel Prince about
thirty. The music ſtopped in the boat alongside.
The King and Prince were entertained with biscuit,
butter, sugar, and sherbet. They went to see the
Colonel's books, with which they were much delighted. The Colonel made the King a present of the
Alcoran, the Bible of the Mahometans, in their own
language, richly bound in London, worth four hundred
rupees. The king invited the Colonel to his country
house, about ten miles diſtant. He promised to
come next day. The Colonel invited Mr Mathison,
the super-cargo, from on board the *Duke of Cumberland*,
to accompany him. He was ready by nine o'clock,
went on shore and met the Prince, who accompanied
us. We were in company, the Colonel, Mr Mathison,
the Prince and I, and the Prince's servant, and the
Colonel's black fellow, whom he had to attend him
while in Joanna, and to carry the umbrella, made of
paper, over his head. I had two bottles of rum with
me. We walked up the mountains along the footway
through the fineſt shrubberies. We were two miles
higher than the surface of the sea. Many times we
looked back. The ships looked like small boats on the
river Thames ; and it is impossible to express the
beauty of the scene, or the fine smell of the trees,
fruit, and flowers ; there is not a palanquin or any

carriage on the whole island. The King walks where-
ever he goes, and his people have word about with him.
The King's town lies in a valley, where no white man
had been in the remembrance of any person living
and, had it not been for the *Alcoran*, nor we neither.
The houses were no more than huts, except a few
higher ones for the King and the Prince that had the
King's daughter, his wife, here ; and another where we
came from, and where he has four wives at different
places.

It would have alarmed the inhabitants to see white
people, had it not been known that the Colonel gave
the King a present of the *Alcoran*. We arrived at the
King's house for business. No person can go to the
family houses. The King and Prince of Joanna
received the company kindly. There was plenty of
fruit and lemonade, and I added rum ; for we wanted
refreshment after walking ten miles over the mountains.
There was a bench like a tailor's work-board, covered
with a Scotch carpet, which the King had got in
exchange of trade, and which did well for sitting on.
Governor Rustan came in : he had the command of the
town when the ships lay at anchor. He made a grand
salam, and they all spoke the Moorish language ; his
son had the Colonel's linen to wash. The capital
men's sons at Joanna, when any ships arrive, come on
board, get the passenger's linen to wash, which is
done by their slaves ; they will show you a recom-
mendation from one of the last ship's company.
They charged a dollar for sixty pieces, whether large

or small. In like manner you give a character from your hand, which they show to the next ship's company. They make the linen as white as snow. The King and the Princes tasted the rum, and then put a little in their sherbet. They went away home, and sent a fine curry, both of fish and chickens, and fine rice boiled. The Colonel's servant waited; and I had as much as I could eat, and there was punch enough. It was the best dinner I ever ate. After dinner the Prince and King of Joanna came and sat awhile with the Colonel, and conversed; they spoke English very well; and said that Englishmen and Joanna men were just like brothers. As we had more punch, the Colonel prevailed on the King to drink out of his own cup; the King made each of the two gentlemen a present of a turban of fine muslin, richly mixed with gold and silver; and I had one of an inferior sort; and two young bullocks and two milch-goats were ordered for the Colonel from Joanna. Next morning the Colonel thanked the King of Joanna for his politeness and attention. After conversing, they both withdrew; in half an hour two fine girls came in with a veil over their heads and bodies. When they came in, that was thrown off. They were very richly dressed. I declare they were like a diamond: they made my hair stand on end to see them. I went directly out along with the black men: when I came home I lay down in a little apartment. The girls went off at five in the morning; I came in at six, and got some toddy with the cocoanutters, which we mixed with rum and fruit, and made a breakfaſt about eight. The Prince came to accompany the Colonel. After drinking some toddy, with rum, we set off, dressed in our turbans; the black man carried the gentlemen's hats, and I carried my own. Every person looked at us as we went along, with the two bullocks and the two she-goats behind us. I never enjoyed more happiness in my life than at this time, the walk was so pleasant, and everything agreeable. We walked along where no white man living had been but ourselves. All the people were very desirous so see us. As we walked along, the Colonel made a remark on our turbans; the Colonel's was rich blue and gold, Mr Mathison's red, rich with silver, and my turban green, with gold at the ends— juſt the colour of the three orders in Great Britain, the garter, the bath, and the thiſtle. It was a little laughable, as the King gave those three colours by chance. The gentlemen conversed as they walked along; they asked the Prince if the King was rich; he answered that the King had ten thousand dollars in ready money; he told how pleasant it was in the south part of the island; and that there he had one of his wives, and that in Raham Island he had another. This lay on the eaſt side of Joanna, where he had cattle. ﹡

We arrived at Joanna town at twelve o'clock; the Colonel sent one bullock and the two milch-goats as a present to Commodore Smith, and the other bullock to Captain Savage of the *Duke of Cumberland*. As the boat was not ready to carry the two gentlemen on board the *Lord Camden* to dine, they walked about, and, to put off time, went into the Mosque. We all put off our shoes, which is the custom. The two gentlemen were in scarlet, which looked very well with the turbans. On the passage the Colonel gave me an old scarlet coat. I cut off the skirts and made it a short coat, which with the turban looked better than theirs, more like that of a sepoy officer. The people came and admired us much at seeing us go into the Mosque. We got on board to dinner. As I spoke so much about the curry, twelve of us made a party to dine on shore next day. As the King's silversmith was on board, we asked him to make some curry, to which he agreed. The Commodore's cook, and servant, ship-carpenter, ship-steward, the boatswain, and some midshipmen, were in our party. We all walked a great deal, and then had an excellent dinner of curry and rice.

Next day the Colonel and Mr Mathison went up the valley to see the grand cascade which falls over the rock, a quarter of a mile perpendicular height, one of the finest in the world. Before nine they went on shore, as they wanted to catch a dish of trout. As both the Commanders were to dine on shore that day in their marquees under the cocoa-nut trees, the men were all got well with good fresh provisions. They had got wood and water on board, and all was ready for sailing, only waiting for a fair wind. I went to the Commanders when they were angling under the cascade, where they had great success, having caught a large dish of trout for their mess. I carried brandy, and the gentlemen made a boy climb up the trees to throw down some cocoa-nuts. They mixed brandy with the cocoa-nut milk and drank it. They arrived at the dining-place at one o'clock with their fish. The two marquees were facing one another; and while they were at dinner the gentlemen drank to one another. There were two French horns between the marquees playing at dinner, and the evening was spent with pleasure. The Prince came after dinner and sat awhile, and the black people came and danced to the gentlemen. It was a dance with cudgel-playing, very merry.

Next day the Colonel was to dine on board the *Duke of Cumberland*, with Captain Savage and Mr Mathison: they both went to angle as before, and I followed them with liquor. At one o'clock they were on board at dinner; they told of the sport, and how John always brought them a Scotch dinner—all drinking but no eating. I dined with the Captain's servant. I told them of our journey up to the King's town. The wind came round to the south-west, and Commodore Smith made a signal for sailing. The company broke up: the Colonel went into the boat, and I after him. In half an hour we were under sail, with a fine wind.

Next day, when we were sailing with a brisk wind and a rough sea, the Commodore called me after breakfaſt, to cut his hair and put it in order to go on shore at Bombay. At that inſtant a Scotch boy fell overboard. The alarm was given. The Commodore called: "Down with the sails—throw the hen-coop overboard." All hands were looking over. He was a boy about sixteen; and, as he was a fine swimmer, he put off his clothes and got on the hen-coop, where he sat and held faſt till the ship was ſtopped and a boat let down. He was then a mile behind: the men went for him in the boat; took him in, fixed a rope to the hen-coop, and brought him on board. He loſt his clothes, but he had enough given him by the gentlemen. We went on with a fair wind, and when we were on the coaſt of Malabar one morning Captain Savage sent the Commodore twelve hot rolls for breakfaſt, and a fine salad for dinner. The salad grew in two little gardens on the hind-corners of the poop. As we were sailing down the coaſt of Malabar, we saw a fight at sea between the fleets of Hyder Ali and the Mahrattas. We saw the firing very well for two hours. Hyder Ali's fleet ſtruck to the Mahrattas. Our two ships at this time were within three miles of each other. We arrived at Bombay the middle of September, after all the rains were over.

General Pimble received the Colonel at the Marine House, and took him to his country house at Maſtegan, a mile from Bombay Town, and close to Messigan Village. The house ſtood on a hill almoſt surrounded by sea. General Pimble was then Commander-in-Chief at Bombay. The Colonel sent a sepoy for me and the baggage and to show me the way to the Commander-in-Chief's house.

Next day the Colonel went to Paralle, in the country, to wait on Governor Hodges, and the day following he took the command of all the sepoys on the Bombay eſtablishment. There were four battalions which amounted to nine thousand men. We were three weeks at General Pimble's, which was of service to me to learn the ways of the place. The General kept a great deal of company, and had a great number of servants. I waited every day at table. It is an old saying and a true one; " Go where you will, whatever place, you will find an acquaintance sooner or later by chance". The General's valet was a German, Adam la Plue. When I was at the German Spa with Mr Crauford, he was footman to Lady Spencer, but on some account he was obliged to retreat to India as a soldier. He put himself down as a hairdresser, and the General took him out of the ranks. He and I slept and eat together. Now I was out of livery, and he in livery. One morning the Colonel said : " John, bring my clothes and dress me for the ball; I dine with the General in town at his own house, and we shall dress after dinner." As I was carrying my bundle, and Adam passing me on horseback, I asked the favour of him to carry it before him, for it was very hot, but he would not. I waited dinner, and in the evening the two gentlemen dressed in one room.

I went that night to see their manner at the ball, for the servants in India are excellent and sober. When the Colonel came home, he said: " John, my hair ſtands up as well as when I went out, and all the other gentlemen's hair is down." I said: " Sir, the people here don't know how to use the pomade " ; for I had contrived to ſtiffen the pomatum with waxen candles. He answered : " If you like, you may get a great deal of money here by cutting gentlemen's hair ; and, John, as I have got the command of the Sepoys, I shall give a ball to the gentlemen and ladies at the Marine House next week, and I shall desire the favour of Buckthergee, the General's ſteward, to buy in all the things for supper, as you are a ſtranger. When it comes in you muſt order the supper, and the General's cooks will make it ready ; and I have hired Wanella, a Persian servant to assiſt you." " Very well, sir ", I replied ; " I shall do my endeavour to set everything out to the beſt purpose." I went and looked at the table-room, and then asked Buckthergee, who was a Mahometan, and had a servant of his own, what things he could send me. He gave me an idea of different things. I begged of him to send four turkeys, two cocks, and two hens, the two cocks roaſted, set round with sausages, and the two hens boiled, with oyſter sauce. I made out a bill of fare for supper, of fifty things, on a long piece of paper, after the manner of Europe. I made a circle round a crown, a half-crown, a shilling, and round a farthing. I wrote the name of every dish as it was to ſtand on the table, and I gave it to Silveſter, the head cook, to put up in his cook-room. I set the table and the side-tables. I had two silver *épargnes* full of sweetmeats, and three cryſtal ſtands with syllabubs and jellies, in a row on the middle of the table, with three rows of plates with fruits and deserts from top to bottom. I was determined to exert myself. On the afternoon of the ball I dressed myself in a green silk waiſtcoat, double-breaſted, with sleeves mounted with gold, like a jacket. When the cook asked a queſtion, he came to me to read the bill, and an excellent supper he did dress. The General's butler and I made negus and punch, and served out the wines. All the black men seemed very well pleased to assiſt in anything they were desired to do, and seemed surprised to see an Englishman have the command. As servants, there were only two Europeans in the island, Adam Le Plue with the General (he did nothing but take care of his maſter's clothes and dress his hair) and another with Colonel Gordon from Lisbon (he dressed his maſter and took care of the liquors, but to provide for a table he knew nothing). Colonel Keating, Colonel Egerton, Mr Ramsay and Mr Hornsby's butlers came. They were Moors. The General's butler was an Asiatic Roman Catholic. He desired me to ask them. I went and desired them to assist me that night, as I was a stranger and come to remain amongst them. They made a salam, and said they were happy to be at my service the whole night ; so I gave them some tea and cakes, but they could not eat with me, or drink liquor.

When the table was trimmed, and all ready, before supper the black men admired it, and said: "Your table looks like a diamond, Steward." I lost the name of Macdonald that night, and got the name of Steward ; for a head-servant in India is always called 'Steward'. The company assembled, the dancing went on ; and, when my fellow-servant, Wanella, the Persian, was taking round some negus to the ladies, he heard Miss De la Guarde ask the General what gentleman that was in the green and gold. "Madam, that is John Macdonald, Colonel Dow's servant." The broad gold lace, though tarnished by day, shone among so many lights. At twelve the supper was ready, and carried up by the servants that came to wait on their masters. The upper-servants I mentioned before put the supper on the table. I held the bill of the supper in my hand, to show them to put everything in its place. Everything was done at a word ; and they were more happy to be directed by me than by one of their own people. The company sat down, and I put the bill before the Colonel. The gentlemen said they never saw such a supper in Bombay, nor things better conducted ;

and the gentlemen were well pleased that the black servants saw a white man could order a supper as well as either of them, or better. When supper was over, the bill of fare was handed about from one lady to another, and they said : "Certainly, this Englishman is a very good servant." The company broke up at four in the morning. When I was putting the Colonel to bed, he said : "John, I'll be damned but you conducted yourself vaſtly well at this ball, and with judgment ; and the gentlemen give you a great character, and they say you have the beſt method of any with the black men." I answered : "Sir, I am very glad I have done right, and given satisfaction." After this I was very much respected by the black men. The Colonel gave one thousand rupees for a saddle-horse, and bought two horses for his chariot, all ſtallions ; he hired a firſt and second coachman, and bought two slaves, one for the kitchen and the other to help Wanilla and me. As the Colonel had taken a house, he went to housekeeping. He got Captain Savage's second cook, a black man, an American. The Colonel asked the favour of Mr Mathison, the super-cargo of the *Duke of Cumberland*, to be in the house with him as a companion, till the ship was to sail for Macoa, which was about three months. The servant Mr Mathison had from England got to be a writer, therefore I dressed him. The Colonel and Mr Mathison got four coolies each, to carry their palankin. The Colonel had a massall to carry the umbrella by day and the flambeau by night, and a pair to run before the chariot or palankeens with swords drawn in their hands : so this was our family, without a maidservant.

As my master made his fortune in Bengal and was a single man, he did not mind money ; therefore he kept the best house in Bombay. The principal people dined with one another in their turn. The custom is, where they dine, they sup ; and there was nothing to provide at home. As the country is very hot, my master told me to buy everything that was wanting in the house. He got a list of the prices of everything for the house and for the use of the horses from Buckthergee, the Steward. I paid every servant their wages the first day of the month always ; if any did not fill their place, I turned him away, and hired another in his place, without acquainting the Colonel. Our house was called the first in Bombay for hospitality. The Colonel invited the Commander-in-Chief and his Lady, and the first gentlemen and ladies in town, to dinner and supper. The dinner was admired much, and the ladies said : " It is very odd we cannot have such a dinner at our own houses : yet there is not one woman in this house ! " And the General said after dinner : " Good God, how handy this young man is turned out ! " When I was putting the Colonel to bed, he told me so, and gave me great applause ; and next day he gave me three suits of clothes, trimmed with gold.

In December Commodore Sir John Lindsay arrived at Bombay, with the King's ships-of-war under his command. He sent his Steward and the Stewards of the captains under his command to know the price of things in the island, the same as I learned from Buckthergee. According to cuſtom, at Chriſtmas the Governor gave a dinner to all the gentlemen in the island, about two hundred and fifty, and the same on the firſt day of the New Year, and all we English servants waited, for there was a great many in Sir John Lindsay's fleet. We all dined together, and each had two bottles of wine allowed him. The time of the year that is called winter in Europe was spent in a jovial manner,—in visiting, balls, and entertainments. At this time an evil thought came into the mind of General Pimble, I believe for himself as well as for others. He wanted all the officers to wear boots on duty. It was againſt the caſte or religion of the Gentoo officers to eat beef or wear their skins, even calves' or sheep-skins. Some of the principal officers waited on the General, to tell him they could not possibly comply with his order to wear boots that were made of the skins of those creatures, which was entirely againſt their caſte or religion; if they did, they would lose their caſte and be deprived of the company of their relations. The General insiſted that they should wear the boots or give up their commissions. They got three days to consult with their friends and return an answer. They put up prayers to God, and hoped that God of his goodness would not impute the sin to them nor their children, but to the person who was the cause of their wearing boots of skins of those beasts which was entirely against their religion. The prayers were put up in the pagodas at Bombay. They told him they had determined to wear the boots, according to his desire. " Since ", said they, " God has sent you from Europe to give us disturbance concerning our religious principles and to deprive us of our friends' company and the benefits of our religion, we will submit to God and your Excellency." So they took leave and went home. In three weeks the General was smitten with the dropsy, and never recovered. About this time my master gave a dinner to Sir John Lindsay and his officers. The Colonel, Sir John Lindsay, Andrew Ramsay, Esq., and Mr Patterson, Secretary to Commodore Lindsay made an appointment to go to the hot-wells at Dillanagogue, in the Mahrattas country inland, over against Bombay. They were to go in the month of April. Commodore Watson and other gentlemen were to go in another party to the same place. The General was getting very ill, his disorder growing worse every week. The advice of his physicians, Tennant, Bond, and Richardson, was to go to Bencoot, one of our settlements, a fine airy situation as any in India. People are sent there just as gentlemen are sent from England to Lisbon or the South of France, for the benefit of their health. The General went to Bencoot ; and Colonel Gordon was left in command, as being the senior officer. Commodore Watson, his family and

party, were gone to Dillinagogue. Commodore
Watson belonged to the Honourable East India
Company. The Colonel and his party were preparing ; and we set off in a large boat, with sails, across the
sea, and entered the great river of Tannah, with a
vessel following us with all the necessaries for an
empty house, servants, two havaldars, or sepoy serjeants,
twelve sepoys, with their arms, four palankins, with
eight men for each, four saddle-horses, with their
keepers. We had plenty of provisions with us for
two days in the boats. I was greatly delighted, and
thought it was a pleasant thing to live under the
East India Company.

We passed Salsette, Carranjaw, and the beautiful
country, and the banks of the river. The people
came in numbers to see us. The country people
brought us some of them milk, others fruit. Before
we came opposite the city and fortification of Tannah,
which is near the banks of the river, the Colonel sent
his servant Rustan on shore, with a message to the
Governor, Rummagee Punt, for a passport. We
waited three hours for it. We could not stir, nor go
near the fort ; if we had, we should have been fired at.
The gentlemen sent their respects, and that they
would do themselves the honour to wait on his
Excellency on their return. The passport came when
they were at dinner. We set sail, and passed the
towers and walls of the fort in the afternoon.
Thousands of people were looking at us and the

sepoys over the walls. Our sepoys had new clothes, and all red and blue turbans. The two havaldars were like two officers, two likely young men, Mahometans. In the evening, when the tide turned, we ſtopped. The gentlemen drank punch, and sang till they fell asleep in the cabin. In the day, two of Mr Ramsay's servants used the firſt and second French horns, which were very pleasant on the river. I was the only white servant there. My fellow-servant, Ruſtan, told me he never heard of a white servant there before. Sir John Lindsay's valet, a German, was left sick at Bombay. His name was Longchamps, after-wards a great man at Newmarket.

In the evening we landed at the Bundy, a town, from whence we were to go by land to the hot wells. We were all night at a rich Moorman's house, who was often at Bombay on business. He let Mr Ramsay have an apartment in his house, for himself and the gentlemen. At the Bundy, a pleasant town, we left the river to go by land. The Moorman at whose house we were had a great many wives ; and one Sally Percival, a black girl, who had gone along with us, had an opportunity to go in where they were. She told them the English gentlemen had a great desire to see them, and begged to let her undraw the curtain on the inside the window. When the maſter, Afdalla, was gone out a little they went and had a sight, by looking through a window. They did not ſtay a minute, for fear of his return. One gentleman said : " They are pretty " ; another said : " They are richly dressed." " I wish we had them here ", said another. This Sally Percival whom I have mentioned lived with a gentleman who had gone home to Europe. He gave her her freedom, and a great deal of money. Afterwards she lived with Dr Percival, by whom she had a son ; but the Doctor died, and left a great deal of money to Sally and the little boy. By this time she was worth between four and five thousand pounds sterling. She had a town-and country-house in the island of Bombay. Dr Tennant and Mr Ramsay were her trustees.

In the morning, after the gentlemen were dressed, I and Rustan and Bigo, two Persian men belonging to Sir John Lindsay, set out on horseback up a valley about fifteen miles long. The gentlemen were to follow in their palankeens, and Sally Percival along with them. At the top of the valley were the hot wells, surrounded by the mountains. The valley was very pleasant, about two miles broad, with a small serpentine river on our right hand. As we rode along we saw a large fort on the top of the hill that contained a thousand men ; and there was another on our left hand, on the top of a very high mountain, near Dillinagogue. When we came to Dahoo, a village half-way to the Wells, we stopped to have some milk and cocoa-nuts. My horse picked up a stone in his shoe. I knocked it out with another stone, which made my hands dirty. I went to wash them in the puddle that lay near the well of the village. At that time a farmer's daughter came for water, a pretty girl, a Gentoo. She had her slave-girl with her, to carry the water home. She was sorry to see me washing my hands in the dirty water; therefore she poured water on my hands out of the pitcher. I washed my hands and dried them with my handkerchief. Then I made her a low salaam, and took hold of her hand. A freeman's daughter at Bombay would not have done so for any money—they are kept at so great a distance from the English. When she went away, I told Rustan she was a fine girl. He said: "She was very well pleased that you made her a grand salaam before her slave girl. She thinks we are all your servants, by your having that fine gold-laced hat, and gold on your coat." Most people of the village came to see us, whilst we were drinking our milk. After we left this place, as we pursued our journey there were some mares feeding. Our horses, being stallions, were like mad things after the mares. They ran after them, so that we could not stop them, and began fighting with one another. We were therefore obliged to throw ourselves from off their backs. Rustan, Bigo and I were never more happy in our lives than when we got safe off their backs. When the three horses' keepers came up, who were a little way behind, they got hold of the horses with great difficulty. We got on horseback again, and arrived at Dillinagogue in the afternoon. A while after the gentlemen arrived. The houses were made and covered with branches of trees. The building of a house would cost eighteen half-crowns. There was no rent to pay ; but when the gentlemen went home before the rains should come, which is about the end of May, the farmers take the house for firewood. There is plenty of fish, fowl, mutton, wild-boar, hares and other provisions cheap. The gentlemen drank the waters, dressed, played at cards, and after dinner slept an hour or two ; then in the afternoon they rode out on horseback, and in the evening played at cards again.

After we had been here some time, the tiger came at night, and paid our hen-house a visit. As it was very easy to break open, he killed the fowls and took them away. After this a sepoy was sent up the tree to shoot him when he came, but he never killed one, as he commonly fell asleep. Two weeks after we came here, a pattamar came with an express of the death of General Pimble at Bencoot, where he was buried. Next express by a pattamar brought an account that the ship that brought the gentlemen that attended the General, in their return to Bombay with Adam La Plue, the General's servant, and the baggage, were attacked by the coolies. On their return home, in the battle the fire of the coolies got into the ship's powder-room, and blew the ship up in the air, and all was lost ; and that Sir John Lindsay's head-cook went to bed at Bombay well at night, and was found dead in the morning. The gentlemen were very sorry, for there were a great many of their friends blown up with the ship.

In three weeks Commodore Watson and his party went home, round the hot wells. This was the pleasanteſt place I ever saw : fine large old trees in abundance, and many rivulets running down from the mountains all round. When we walked at night, we had a ſtick with a rattle on the end of it, to rattle as we went along to frighten the serpents away, for fear we should tread on them. I was very much delighted here with one thing : at Dillinagogue there was a tank where the Gentoos bathe themselves, and the women in particular. At the end of the tank is a piece of rising ground, with a cross fixed twelve feet high, where a prieſt sits moſt days, naked as he was born. When the women come to enter the bath, they make the prieſt a grand salaam. They have a shift on when they enter the water. When a young girl, who has been betrothed for some years is going home to her husband (for they marry very young and go to their husband's house from their father's at twelve or thirteen) and on that occasion goes to take the bath, with two married women behind her, she makes a grand salaam to the prieſt, and kisses his private parts, hoping he will pray that they may have children. I took a great delight in going to see those ceremonies.

After being five weeks at this place, we returned home towards the end of May. We went down the river to Tannah. The gentlemen slept in their barge on the river, and next day sent a message to the governor, to let him know they would wait on him. Rummagee sent his compliments, with a message that he would be glad to see the gentlemen. He ordered a troop of horse and a company of foot to attend them into the castle. Rummagee paid great respect to Colonel Dow, because he was the Commandant of the sepoys. He was as much honoured at Tannah as a King in Europe, because he commanded the black troops and spoke the language of the country.

When the gentlemen left the castle, the next place they went to see was the Portuguese or Roman-Catholic Church. I followed the gentlemen there. I was very well dressed; and the two havaldars, or sepoy serjeants, were with me. When we came near the church, the horse and foot stood under arms. When they saw us and knew that I was the Commandant's Steward, they sounded the music and beat the drums, to give me two cheers. I took off my hat and made a low bow; and the havaldars made them a grand salaam as we passed the ranks to follow the gentlemen into church. When the Colonel came out of church, he discharged the sepoys and took the horsemen with him. The gentlemen were going two miles further, to see some figures of the Gentoo Gods cut in the rock on the face of a hill. I had no desire, nor the havaldars, to go on; so we returned, and we met Rustan and Bigo, the two Persian men. I asked them to go into a Roman-Catholic public-house, where I treated them with some Persian brandy. Each cast had a cocoa-nut to drink out of, for they cannot drink with one another. I ordered the land-lord to bring some fruit for each of them. They were all well pleased ; and the master, his wife, and daughter were very happy to see a white Christian visitor. I drank out of their own cup ; and the landlord broiled some fish called Sparling. So we feasted, each religion by itself, till the gentlemen returned to the barge to dinner. The Colonel gave the horsemen forty rupees, and to the footmen twenty rupees ; so they were dismissed very well pleased. The gentle-men played at cards and drank punch in the evening. Mr Ramsay's two servants played on the first and second French horn, which very much entertained the inhabitants. Early the next morning the tide carried us down the river into the salt water, and the same day we arrived safe in Bombay.

In the month of August, 1770, General Wedder-burne arrived at Bombay from Europe, with a com-mission from the Honourable East India Company to take the command of the troops in Bombay ; and General Pimble was to take the command at Madras if he had lived. General Wedderburne went to Parnell House in the country, to wait on Governor Hodges, with his commission ; and next day he took the command of the troops in Bombay Green. This year was spent very agreeably between the King's and the Company's servants at Bombay.

In the beginning of 1771, Sir Eyre Coote arrived at Bombay, on his way to Europe from Madras. He ſtayed some time, and was entertained by all the firſt people of rank in the island. There was a grand review of all the troops belonging to Bombay and Old Woman's Island, where the grand encampment was formed by General Coote and General Wedderburne. Sir Eyre Coote was going to Europe overland, through the deserts of Arabia; and my maſter, who did not like Bombay, asked leave of Governor Hodges to accompany Sir Eyre to England. His requeſt was granted. When he came home, he told me he was to go to England, and that he was to have a sale in two days of everything that he had. " But you muſt get my clothes, plate, books and maps packed up; give a grand dinner to the Council and all the general officers." I had been ill a great while, and the fatigue of this dinner made me worse. I foolishly had got the disorder of the country, and had not applied to a proper person at firſt. I told the Colonel I was very ill, and he desired me to go to Dr Richardson. When I went to see the doctor, he told me if I went with the Colonel I should lose my life. I went to the Colonel and told him. He said: " I am very sorry; then I muſt take Stephen, the cook, with me, I can do no other." I went to Dr Richardson to ask him if he would take me under his care in the hospital; for as I did not belong to the company, I had no title to the hospital. He said that he would. When I found that he would take me under his care, I sent him the same afternoon a fashionable silver mug that cost me five pounds in St James's Street, London. When the Colonel was going he took me by the hand and said that he had recommended me to Colonel Keating; and that, if he came back, he would take me himself; and he paid me like an emperor. Next day I went into the hospital, and Mr Richardson put me in the first ward; and in every respect treated me as the first person there. I was there six weeks. When I was getting better, Colonel Keating sent a message, whenever I could get out, to come to his house till I got better. I returned for answer that I would; and that I was much obliged to him.

One day, as I was walking out early in the morning on the outside of the gate, Major Pointing, who was exercising the sepoys on the green, when he saw me, called me, and asked me how I did. I told him I was getting well. "Well, John, will you come and live with me when you get better, or come to my house whenever you like?" I told him I was obliged to him, but that Colonel Keating had spoke to me to come to his house. "Then," said he, "you will repent that. You know I have the best right to you, as I have taken your master's place; and, if you serve me, you shall order every thing as you like." I said: "Very well; I shall see and give an answer, sir." We spent our time in the ward very pleasantly; they were gentlemen's sons, midshipmen, or mates; we played at cards for tea, coffee and sugar, and sometimes for our wine that we had in the hospital. So everything was as agreeable as possible. Next morning, when the doctors came round and did their business, Dr Richardson called me out of the ward and asked me if I intended to take a place or go to England. I said I would take a place. "Very well, I shall speak to Governor Hodges to take you for his Steward, as he spoke to me some time ago to get him an European Steward to take care of his clothes, liquors and plate; and if I can get that place for you it will be the making of you; and you may sleep in the hospital or out, which you like." I told him I was much obliged to him. Next day, Mr Mathison, the super-cargo of the *Duke of Cumberland*, came to see me, and to ask me to come to Colonel Keating's house. The ship was returned from Macoa. He slept at Colonel Keating's, as he did at Colonel Dow's, before he went to Surat and Macoa; he was very desirous to have me there on account of having his hair done.

Another circumstance probably made him desirous that I should come to Colonel Keating's. Mr Mathison brought the famous horse Chillabie from Macoa, at this time four years old; he was chained in Colonel Keating's stable by the head and legs. He had killed one Arab at Macoa; and on the passage he had almost killed another; therefore the black man would not go near him. Mr Mathison knew I underſtood horses. I helped Mahomed, the coachman, to break in two mules he sent to Colonel Dow when he went firſt to Juddah. I went to the Colonel's house, and by that ſtep I loſt the beſt opportunity ever offered to me. After I was there, and my things with me, I had not fortitude to come away again. All that I did was to dress their hair and to give orders to the black horse-keepers about the ' mad horse ', as they called him; for I had very little ſtrength after coming out of the hospital. This horse was called after a very rich merchant at Surat, who had eighteen or nineteen ships of his own and a great many English gentlemen in his service. He lived a great while at Bombay for his pleasure. He was a jovial hearty fellow, and broke through the rules of his religion to have company with the English gentlemen and to drink wine. He was a great companion of General Wedderburne's and of the firſt-rate men. He was a Mahometan, and his name was Chillabie. In a few days Mr Richardson sent for me; he said he had spoke to the Governor about me, " and I have given you a great charaᴄᵗer, so that you may go to Parrella as soon as you please ". I said : " Very well, sir ; I am very much obliged to you : I shall go when I have cut and dressed Colonel Keating's hair." When the Colonel was gone to a ball, I told Mr Mathison that the Governor wanted me to live with him. He answered : " If you go to Parrella, you will be con-fined in the country amongſt a parcel of Persians ; besides, the Governor is very changeable in his mind,

and puts his whole confidence in Gentoo Bramins."
He went and told Colonel Keating ; and next morning
after breakfaſt Mr Mathison asked me if I went to the
Governor or would I hire myself to the Colonel. I
said : " Gentlemen, whatever you think beſt." The
Colonel said : " John, your maſter recommended you
to me, and I will give you as much as Mr Hodges ;
and everyone in my house knows you. I will give you
forty guineas a year, my old clothes, and bed, board,
and washing. You will have charge of everything
in my house. Bapu buys everything for the house,
but he is not always here ; and he likes you very
much." I agreed to ſtay ; and the Governor was a
little displeased. Next time the Governor had the
Colonel to dine with him at Parella ; and in conversation after dinner with the company he said :
" Colonel Keating, I do not like you because you are so
partial to the Scots." " I cannot help that, Governor
Hodges, for I think when I meet Scotchmen that are
good, they are the beſt of men." Colonel Keating
was Commandant of artillery and principal engineer ;
he had as many attendants about him as a royal or a
noble prince in England. Bapu was his head-servant ;
he had a plantation of his own, and a large family. As
he was above taking wages, the Colonel made him a
present now and then. Next to him were two Tindalls,
petty officers, and five Lascars, as servants, excused
from duty. Two would come in the morning, and
two to dinner, and two to supper, juſt as they liked ;
there was always enough of them and the Colonel did

not mind which: three cooks and three slave-boys always in the house. A Tindall's command of twelve Lascars on guard night and day at the gate; and an English coachman and three black helpers in the ftables. When there was a large company at dinner, there was Bapu, and Baba, and Sheek, and five Lascars, all in Turbans, besides our slave-boys and ftrange servants, all waiting at dinner. Bapu was over us all when he attended; when he did not, then I was headman. In regard of dressing the Colonel and taking care of his clothes, that was to myself. I took care of the side-table, and Bapu took notice and sent me wine. He never waited at table, but would sit down in the fender, come in to see what the Colonel wanted, put down the dinner, and take it off. The Colonel's perquisites amounted to as much as the pay of the Commander-in-Chief. He had as many men at work under him, at cutting down rocks and building new fortifications, as coft one hundred thousand rupees per month; and, when he came in his palankeen after breakfaft to see some hundreds of men at work, he was taken more notice of than the King of England at St James's on a court day. There was one Captain Macneal, an engineer, an Argyleshire gentleman, who assifted the Colonel in his works. When I came I took a little trouble off his hands, in regard of receiving all the Colonel's money, as I was always in the way. I had a drawer that ran on wheels, to keep the money in. A paper was brought to me to receive so much money. I took care of the paper and gave an account of the

money. When a bill was to be paid, the Colonel put
his name to the bottom, I received the bill and paid
the contents, which lessened Captain Macneal's
trouble at home. When Bapu was to have a sum of
money, he brought the order, and I paid the money
to him. I took care of the papers and what I paid I
marked in my book.

In two months after I was there the Colonel was
taken with a putrid fever. He was so extremely ill
that for twelve nights I never went to bed nor pulled
off my clothes: he had no nurse but me. The
doctors were all called for. On the tenth day he was
given over: his friends were called, and his will was
made and read to him in my hearing. At twelve
o'clock he said : " Now, my friends, leave me to rest."
After the gentlemen had supped, they went home,
and all the black men were asleep, for they are natur-
ally very sleepy ; and I lay on the bed with the Colonel
wetting his lips with a feather while he was motion-
less. At three I took a looking-glass to put over his
mouth to see if there was any life. By the glass I
found there was life. I knew there would be a change
at four in the morning, because, at four, the morning
before, he changed from better to worse. As I
expected, so it pleased God, that from four he received
strength more and more, as you would see the sea
flow. The gentlemen sent in the morning to know
if the Colonel was dead or not. But, to their great
surprise and comfort, they saw him sitting up in the

bed to breakfaſt. At nine o'clock his friends were very
happy, for they never expeɔted to see him in life
again. The doɔtors said I had done great things, and
they recommended me to go to bed; which I did.
The Colonel got out of danger; but his disorder was
not gone. He changed his bed from one room to
another. And I slept in the room wherever he went.

By this time Governor Hodges was taken ill, and his
illness increased; and the Colonel was so happy that he
was better that he told me one morning, with much
satisfaɔtion, that he dreamed in the night he was
playing at cards with Death, and beat Death. I
answered: "Then, sir, you will certainly get the
better of your illness." His disorder turned to an
ague. He went to his country house at Randal
Lodge. It ſtood on the side of Malabar Hill. He
was there two months. From thence he went to Mr
Ramsay's at Mayan, where he remained one month;
and afterwards to Mr Jarvis's house in the woods.
Here we remained three weeks; then we went back to
Mr Ramsay's again for a change. By this time the
Governor was got so ill that he was desired to go to
Bencoot by his physician, where General Pimble died
and was buried; this made my maſter afraid.
Governor Hodges also was at Bencoot till he died.
His remains were brought to Bombay; he had a very
grand burial; he was laid in the church. The
Colonel came to town again for a month; but there
was so much company to diſturb him that he went to

Randal Lodge; but the putrid fever ſtuck about him ſtill. After all the doctors could do for him he muſt go to Bencoot for the benefit of the air. A vessel was procured and everything got ready. The Colonel took me, the two Tindalls, Baba and Sheek, two cooks, two peons to run before him, one to carry the umbrella and the flambeaux; and six hay-malls to carry the palankeen.

We set sail early in the morning, and with a fair wind arrived at Fort Victoria, where the Eaſt India Company had one hundred and twenty as fine Sepoys as ever I saw, besides their officers and non-commissioned officers. The firſt gunner was born at Aberdeen in Scotland; he had been there fifteen years, and was as black with the heat as the Sepoys. The chief was Mr Cheap. The caſtle and Mr Cheap's house ſtood on a high hill near the sea, and a large river. It is a beautiful country, and a number of different fruit trees grow along the face of the hill. These sepoys had nothing to do but to mount guard at the Chief's gate. A fine easy life they led. We had many sorts of fish, chickens. mutton, lamb, and several other sorts of provisions. We lived very well. There were four gentlemen, the Colonel, Mr Cheap, Mr Forbes, and Mr Arden. They went out in the afternoon, the Colonel in his palankeen, and the gentlemen on horseback. As for me, I walked where I would for my pleasure, with my little sepoy called Toby. The Colonel let me have him for what I wanted. Wherever he went he was called my little sepoy. All he had to do for the Colonel was to clean a pair of shoes, clean the night-pan, to do what I wanted, and to walk out with me. The Colonel reviewed the sepoys, and had two of them flogged for sleeping on guard. It was only to teach them to know their duty. The Colonel told Mr Cheap that Seedy might come and take the fort without firing a gun. Seedy was a Sovereign Prince, whose country lay near ours, and Fort Victoria would have been of great service to him.

The Colonel got a great deal better by the air of Bencoot and by taking the bark. When the Colonel was three weeks at Bencoot, he had a desire to go up the river forty miles to the hot wells, to take the bath. The name of the place where the wells are is Darygan. The Colonel went in Mr Cheap's barge. I am going to mention one remark that was made by General Pimble's lady at Bombay, at dinner. The day we set sail for Bencoot, when she was speaking to the ladies about my master, she said: " General Pimble went for his health to Bencoot, with Adam la Plue his servant, and never returned. The Governor went, and he died. Now we will see what will become of Colonel Keating and John Macdonald." I will mention another thing before we go up the river, which may not be disagreeable. The barge contained the four gentlemen, myself, and Baba and Sheek, the two non-commissioned officers, as worthy fellows as ever lived. Their business was to prepare for the table ; they never cleaned a knife—all the dirty work was done by the coolies that carried the palankeens. Every one had his business ; and, according to their caſte they eat together. The Moormen could not eat with the Gentoos, nor the Gentoos with the Moormen. Baba and Sheek were Mahometans, and Mr Cheap's man also, and the Gentoos at dinner by themselves. Our two cooks and Toby and the other two gentlemen's servants dined together, and I by myself when the gentlemen had done : where they dressed their food under a tree they drew a circle round, and none of the other could come within that line. Before the Colonel's Lady went to England (for at this time she was in London about business, and knew nothing of his illness) she asked the favour of Bapu, Baba, and Sheek, to bring their wives to see her, and she would treat them with fruits and sweet-meats. Bapu made answer : " Madam, we are much obliged to you for your invitation, but we cannot do this : to let our wives visit any European, nor let them visit us ; if we did we should lose our caſte, and be despised by our relations and every one of our religion." Our Lady's maid, Sylvia, who was a Malabar girl, had been to see them at their houses ; and she said that Bapu's wife had as many bangles and jewels as coſt four or five hundred pounds, for he was very rich ; but Baba and Sheek were poorer.

We prowed up the beautiful river of Marr in the cooly boats, sometimes using a sail, and at other times oars on each side. It was very pleasant—moſtly very high hills, covered with fine trees of different sorts, rivulets running down at different placcs, and the mangoes hanging on the trees, and other fruits in our view. It was a beautiful scene, as we sailed along, to see the rocks, hills, and trees, and the birds of different kinds. We arrived at Darygan next morning. The place where the wells ſtood was level, and about two miles round, almoſt surrounded by mountains and groves. The waters were as hot as at Bath in England. The Colonel went into the bath early in the morning, and in the afternoon the gentlemen went out in their palankeens : and then I took the bath, to cure me of my late illness. The gentlemen employed their time here in the same manner as Colonel Dow and his party did at the hot wells at Dillinagogue. The citron trees grew in plenty before our house and round the valley, and the fine large fruit hung on the trees in abundance. The country-people minded them no more than a frog-ſtool. The Colonel had a great many preserved in jars, and taken to Bombay. As this was a Gentoo country, there happened to be some grand holidays, not yearly but upon a particular occasion, which only happens very seldom. Monday was the day to draw the people together. In the great grove the Gentoos meet, dance in different poſtures, and throw a holy red powder on one another. They are dressed with flowers, particularly the women. They eat fruits and sweetmeats. Baba and Sheek were glad to see this fête as well as I. I asked Baba what that ſtage was

for, six feet high and as much square. At the end of
the stage is a large post, eighteen feet high, with
another of an equal length or more, fixed on the top
of the post properly with an iron bolt; so that the one
across runs round like a weather-cock with ease. Sheek
said: Mr John, you will see the grand ceremony
to-morrow." Next day the fête was grander than the
day before, with music, dancing, dress and feasting. A
great many of the gentlemen Gentoos came from the
the city of Marr, and amongst them one very rich,
and a great and good man. He had been married
years, and had no children. I was told prayers had
been put up by the Bramins in the pagodas; at last
he had an only son. In return, he publicly goes
through a torment in honour of his Creator, and the
pure and undefiled Gentoo religion; and his name is
handed down to posterity amongst the worthy as a
saint, and his family respected.

When the operation was to begin, he was seated on
a table, under one of the ends of the cross-poles; an
incision is made in each side, under his ribs, to let in
each hole a smooth iron hook, like those that let down
a butt of beer to a cellar in London, with a string from
the rope that draws him up, round the breast, to keep
him from pitching forward, and to keep him in the
same position. With the irons in his side, he is drawn
up in a moment with a pulley. When he is up, there
is one over him who crosses a rope to hold him there.
His hands and feet are tied that he cannot stir. But

take notice, there are weights on the other end of the crosspole, to balance the person who is drawn up and he who fixes him. So the music is playing, some are crying, others praying for him to get through his misery. At the other end of the pole a rope is fixed, which a man takes hold of and runs him round three times. Whenever he came to the same place, they gave him a cheer; so he had three cheers when he had gone round three times. He was taken down in a moment, a cordial given him, his wounds were dressed and he was carried home in triumph, with beating of drums and music playing. Those who remain behind dance in different companies.

At the top of the grove were the figures of their gods. First was Ram, a man drawn with ten heads and twenty arms, to denote wisdom and strength; with a company of men and women dancing round him, like the ring in Greenwich Park. Next was the Gunness, a man with four arms, and an elephant's head, to denote great wisdom and power. Next was Drougah and his wife; and, on the left of all Mafassoor, a man. There was the Globe of the Earth, the Ox, which is in all their pagodas, the Dove and the Serpent also, and the Turtle. I went home and the first time I saw Vistenorgee, a Gentoo, who was the Colonel's purvoo, or head-clerk, I asked him what was the meaning of all the figures I saw might be. He said Ram was their principal agent between them and God; when he was on earth he had conversation with God, and whatever he said was a law with God ; and how he beat and destroyed kings ; and he gave us this country to live in. By what Vistenorgee told me I found the Gentoos were the descendants of the children of Abraham, by Keturah, whom he sent into the east country to push their fortune and to be out of the way of his son Isaac. Whenever you meet a Gentoo they will say : " Ram, Ram "—that is to say : " God bless you." By what I could understand of what he told me, Ram is for Abraham, Drougah and his wife for Isaac and Rebecca, and Gunness is in remembrance of Jacob, of his wisdom and power with God. The Ox they worship as being the custom in the East at that time. The Dove and the Serpent, to show you to be wise as a serpent and harmless as a dove. The Earth, in remembrance of their forefather, Adam and Eve, who had the whole world under their command. The Turtle, to show you to be satisfied with plenty and with poverty, as the turtle can live in the plentiful sea, and out of his element, on dry land. Mafassoor they look on as a wicked being, so they worship him for fear while they live, and, when dead, deceive the demon, by burning the body and throwing the ashes in water that he may not have it. The Gentoos never indulge unruly lust, nor run into any excess of wickedness, but keep in every respect to the form of their religion. If God approved of the conduct of the Rechabites, who would not obey Jeremiah, who was sent from God with a message, but their father's old commands (*Jeremiah*, xxxv), how much more shall he excuse those Gentoos, who never had the Bible to go by or direct them ? The Colonel was getting better every day, by drinking the waters and taking the bath, so that he was in good spirits, and I was very happy in my own mind that he was recovering, and that I should have the pleasure of his returning to Bombay in perfect health ; he eat very hearty, and drank moderately, and everything was agreeable.

The gentlemen went out four miles in their palankeen. In the evening they played at cards and were merry, and all the attendants were happy with one another ; the black men would have done anything to oblige me, owing to my humility and good temper, though I say it myself. I gave them onions and gee, and curry stuff to dress their victuals, whenever they asked me for any, for I had enough and could buy whenever I pleased. They liked me so much that they would have done anything to deliver me out of trouble if I had been in any ; and they said : " Mr John, you are a very good man ;· God is very good to you." I paid every man his board-wages on Monday morning—every set by themselves. I paid the Havaldar and he paid the sepoys. One day I took notice of the heat as I was walking by the river-side, when the gentlemen were asleep. The cattle lay down in the water. The crows stretched out their wings on the trees to cool themselves, and panting for breath. I went into the room where the Colonel was asleep, and looked at the thermometer, which was up at ninety-four. I took it and hung it under the mango-tree to have the natural air of the country. I observed, in half an hour it got up to one hundred and eighteen degrees of heat. I let it ſtand half an hour longer, and it neither ſtirred up nor down. I carried it in again to its place. When the gentlemen got up and went to sit under the mango-tree for the air where I put the thermometer, where they drank tea, I told the Colonel I had been making two experiments when he was asleep. "What were they John?" "I took the thermomenter and hung it under this tree, on the nail; and in half an hour it got up to one hundred and eighteen; I let it ſtand half an hour, but it never ſtirred. Sir, this was half an hour paſt two, and now it is five o'clock." The gentlemen said: "Good God, is it possible!" They were surprised to hear it. "And, sir, I have been making some tea of the citron-leaves of the tree we gathered the citrons off to preserve, and I have it ready." I brought the tea to them, and they liked it much; and said they never taſted finer tea nor anything more pleasant to drink. By this time we had been here four weeks; and I had a great desire to see the city of Marr, about two miles and a half from Darygan, higher up on the other side of the river. After breakfaſt I asked the Colonel to let me go to Marr and see the place. "Certainly, John, if you like; and you may take Baba or Sheek." "Very well, sir; I am obliged to you." I ordered the dinner, and told Sheek and Baba I was going to see

Marr, and that either of them that liked to go might dress themselves. They were both desirous to go; so they drew lots who should go, and Sheek gained; and Baba to be with the Colonel at home. As the palankeen men were not wanted till the afternoon, I took four of them to carry us through the river, and they were very happy to go. I took the Havaldar also; we crossed the water; the road was pleasant. On both sides were little hills covered with trees.

Before we came to the first Chochee, where was a Havaldar, Naigee, and some Sepoys, we saw one of the sepoys running towards Marr. When we came to the Chochee they turned out and made us a salaam, and we returned it. The Havaldar asked us some questions. We answered; and we asked what the sepoys were gone on for. The Havaldar said it was to give notice there was an European coming to the office of the next Chochee; and he sent another sepoy to the Governor to let him know there was an European coming to Marr; but of what station he did not know. I said to Sheek: " It is very odd they took any notice of us." Sheek said: " They think you are a gentleman because you are dressed in scarlet and that fine gold-lace hat. They think you are one of the gentlemen at the hot-wells, Mr John, because there are six of us attending you: in this country they think every one that wears scarlet and gold to be a great man; and we are glad they think so." When we came to the second Chochee, we sat down, because

the Havaldar was a Moorman of Sheek's caſt. We had
toddy to drink; and soon after, a fine young man, a
Jemmetdar or Lieutenant, came from the Governor
to know who I was. Sheek told the Jemmetdar I
was Steward to one Colonel Keating that was at the
hot-wells, and that I was desirous to see the town.
The Jemmetdar returned to the Governor; and at the
same time I went to see the Roman-Catholic Church;
and he came to us again, and told us the Governor
desired him to walk with us. We went to see the
pagodas, the tank for bathing, all the Governor's
horses, and all the elephants and the camels, and to
walk all round the town—which was very pleasant.
The people followed in hundreds to see us. I said to
Sheek: "These pretty girls are very fond to see us."
He said: "Mr John, they never saw a white man
before, one half of those people; and you are a very
fine piĉture. Mr John, the girls are very glad to
see you." We went into a Portuguese house. I
had rice and curry; and I had arrack enough for the
coolies to drink. Sheek had some bread-fish to eat,
but he drank nothing but water. The Roman-
Catholic landlord was very happy; he and I drank
hearty together, and he said that I was the very firſt
white man that ever was in his house. We were very
merry; so I paid and came to the end of the town,
where I gave the Jemmetdar two rupees, and took our
leave. We came home about six o'clock. I told the
Colonel what usage we had. He said the Governor
behaved very much like a gentleman by sending the

officer with you. It was extremely respectful. By the time we were here five weeks the Colonel was got strong and hearty, and was thinking of going home again, and to go over land and not by water. Mr Cheap sent us forty coolies to carry our baggage. It took twenty coolies to carry our provision chest, so we set out from Darygan in the morning, with seventy-five men and boys, four horses, ten bullocks, and two calves. Mr Cheap came two days journey with us and then took the sepoys home with him. We set off early in the morning on account of the coolies. We did not travel in the middle of the day for the heat, but the morning and afternoon the gentlemen rode in their palankeens, so altogether we were like a little army. The country, in comparison, was like a large garden, so many sorts of fine trees, with the fruit hanging on them in plenty. As we had everything with us that was necessary, we furnished our places where we stopped in ten minutes. We commonly stopped where there were a great many shady trees, for we could not go into the people's houses. No Christian is admitted, and there are no inns on the road ; but they would sell us fowls, eggs, fish, milk, and fire-wood, and the cook would set up a pot, or a spit, in a few minutes, and we could buy provender for the horses and cows and set them a eating. The first place we stopped at was a village under large mango-trees. We put our tea-kettle to boil, and set our tea-table and chairs, and there were a hundred, or several hundred, to see them at breakfast, everything about us was so strange to them. They have no chairs, but sit on the ground : my chair was the provision chest, where I had the liquors. We stopped to breakfast about ten, and there was time enough to dress dinner ; we went on the road again after three, and went on till near dark. We pitched at Lowoos, and furnished our house as before ; we lighted up candles, and put the liquor on the table, the Colonel to bed, and the other gentlemen slept in their palankeens. I slept in my hammock, fixed up between two trees.

The gentlemen had a hot dinner and supper, as if they had been at home. When I was marking down the money I laid out, Mr Cheap asked the Colonel if I kept a journal. The Colonel answered : " I believe John keeps a journal of the rupees." This night the gentlemen supped in public ; there was no danger of any rain coming. It was not the rainy season at this time of the year.

I called the gentlemen before four in the morning, and I called Baba and Sheek, and they called the others, for the black men sleep sound. In half an hour we were all off the ground, and we went by the light of the mosal, or flambeau, till day-light. This day we had a mountain to go over three miles high. We got to the bottom or first part of the mountain about nine o'clock. We could get no water on the road. As we were beginning to go up, there was a hole, where there was a little dirty water. I put my handkerchief over the hole, and sucked the water through it, and the other men took the dirty water up with a spoon, and drank it. We got up the mountain with hard work. On the top was the finest sight I ever saw, just like a pleasure-garden, with so many trees and flowers, and the meal was so fine, when we were beginning to go down the other side of the mountain, I was very happy in my own mind to see the sea.

The sun shined very hot upon us ; but, instead of the sea, what we saw two miles below us was a white cloud. The mountain was called Lowoo. When we descended from the mountains, we came into a pleasant valley, where was plenty of water for man and beast. We pitched beside the river of Lowoo, under some very large oak trees. We were all very hungry, for we had come a great way that morning ; we got breakfast as soon as possible, and afterwards we lay on the grass under the trees and slept, and there were plenty of trees to cover the cattle, and plenty of grass to eat.

There was a Gentoo gentleman that dined where we did. He made the gentlemen a present of some fine mangos ; and my master gave him some pens and paper. We had plenty of fine fish, and some fowls dressed here for dinner. The cattle lay down in the river, and we saw a great many Gentoo women of the village washing their clothes opposite to us. There was one thing on our side—we never had anything to pay for our lodging-place, nor for our fruits ; all was free.

We set out after dinner, and at night arrived at a Mahomedan mosque and burying-ground. The burying-ground was very large and pleasant ; therefore the gentlemen made it their common lodging-place, as it was shaded with fine trees. Baba and Sheek were very happy, as the prieſt of the mosque was of their own ſect. We all slept in the churchyard ; the gentlemen slept in their palankeens, and I made my hammock on the grave of a Mahomedan, and slept with pleasure on the grave of a man I never saw. The Colonel desired me to give the prieſt twenty rupees. He put up a prayer for him and all his attendants. We went to sleep ; and the usual time to call was four in the morning. I was the alarm clock ; called Baba and Cheek, and they alarmed the others.

When I was helping the Colonel on with his clothes, I said : " Sir, I have made a miſtake." " What is that, John ? " " Sir, it is only three, inſtead of four." He said : " John, it is a very good miſtake." We set off, and by daylight Mr Cheap and the sepoys went home.

On that day we passed through a fine level country, and passed by three pagodas and some fine villages. The Colonel called me on the road in the morning, and said : " John, I am going to send Baba on with a message to Raggagee Angerry a sovereign prince; he lives on our way to Bombay, and we are now going through his country. It is about twenty-six miles to Cowrie, where he lives ; and I intend to be there all night. I want you to give Baba Mr Cheap's horse as he will go quicker on to the place." I gave Baba the horse and I got on the bullock ; he had very high horns, and they ſtood ſtraight up: so I made a genteel appearance. We travelled till eleven o'clock; then we pitched at the bottom of a mountain, where there was a grove and a fine spring running out of the rock. We breakfaſted there with pleasure, and after dinner, at three, set off for Cowrie in the afternoon.

Raggagee Angerry, when he had received the message, sent three different men on horseback, one after another, to let the Colonel know he was extremely welcome, and that everything should be ready for him and all his attendants. The Colonel sent one of the horsemen back, to let the Prince know he was coming and then ſtop with us. Each of the horsemen wore a spear in his hand, and they rode a fine Arabian horse each.

Towards seven we ſtopped to water our men, horses, bullocks, cows, and calves. I said to the Colonel : " Sir, here is a fine well of water, and fine shady trees "—for I thought we should be late. " This is as pleasant a place as you have been at yet." The Colonel told Mr Forbes and Mr Orpin : " John wants to coax me to ſtay here all night, but I will not be prevailed on ; I shall go on to Cowrie."

We arrived between eight and nine ; when we came near the fortification, I was surprised to see the great elephant between me and the light of the moon. When the Colonel came to the house made ready for him, there were upwards of twenty noblemen and gentlemen to receive him ; each of them saluted him doubly, so that I was in pain for the Colonel till it was over. He went in and conversed with them. They told him the Prince would wait on him in the morning.

There was a Havaldar and his sepoys ordered to mount guard at the Colonel's door, and there was plenty of provision sent us—fish, fowl, rice, curry ſtuff, milk, etc., for all the attendants, and hay and grain for the cattle. We had no hot supper that night, because the cooks were not come up. The gentlemen's two servants were walking after us on the road, with their French horns on their shoulders, and our two cooks along with them. They often ſtopped to eat fruit and, being three miles behind the Jemmetdar, the commanding officer of a garrison, as we came along, took them prisoners, to give them up to us next day ; but at twelve at the night the whole guard fell asleep, and they made their escape, and came up to us in the morning.

This day was certainly the moſt entertaining and pleasant ever seen : the gentlemen breakfaſted under the jerrander, and before them were all the troughs for washing the elephants, and they were cleaned before them. The Colonel said: "One of those creatures could devour us all, and, for all that, they ſtand like lambs to be ruled by their keepers." And the ſtable where six hundred horses ſtood was before the house. The gentlemen went to see the horses and the place where the elephants ſtood.

The elephants were all brought and harnessed before the Colonel. At the desire of their keepers they lay down to be harnessed and to have the chariot put on their backs; and at their desire they got up again.

The place where we were at present was close by the seaside. Each elephant had a petty officer and two men to attend and clean him; and two of them were taken into the fortification that was at the end of the town, where were three thousand men, fine fellows. The elephants came back soon with twelve fine girls, moſt rich and finely dressed. They ſtopped for all the elephants and a troop of horse to attend the Prince to see the Colonel.

The Prince lived in a ſtrong caſtle, on an island in the sea, about half a mile from shore. When high water, the sea came round the island, and when low water a man could walk to the caſtle and not wet his shoes.

The fortification in the island was ſtrongly fortified. About ten o'clock we saw Raggagee Angerry with six elephants and a troop of horse and sepoys, with a band of music along the sands. I told the Colonel the Prince was coming. He turned about to meet him, and the two gentlemen attending the Colonel. The first elephant carried the standard, next the Colonel of the light horse, and after him the Prince, then some of his Lords and gentlemen. When they alighted, the Colonel saluted the Prince and his company, and went into the house, where they conversed for two hours, music playing the whole time. While they were in the house I was admiring the elephants and the horsemen. Each man had a sword by his side, and a spear in his right hand. The Prince made presents to the gentlemen, and said to Sheek : " I think I saw another European dressed in scarlet." " Yes, your highness there is a very good man, Steward to the Colonel ; he pays all the money for the Colonel's attendants and his house-keeping." " Call him in ", said the Prince, " that I may see him." He gave me a turban and a piece of silk worked with gold, and he gave the same to Baba and Sheek. I made a grand salaam and retired. When he was going, the elephants were called up, and fell down on their bellies till the Prince got into his chariot by a ladder, and in like manner did all the other gentlemen. There was only the body of a chariot, set on a thing like a mattress to save the elephant's back, fixed on by a flat chain, girth, crupper, and breast-plate. Each elephant had a driver who sat on his neck, and two servants on his back behind the chariot. When they were all seated on the elephant, they went away in the same order as they came; then the gentlemen sat down in proper form to a good dinner. The people were much entertained by seeing the gentlemen sit on the chairs round a table to dinner, for they themselves have no tables, but sit on a carpet on the floor to eat. After dinner the Colonel of the light horse went with the gentlemen to show them all the gardens, bathing-places for the Gentoos, and the grand Pagoda that Raggagee Angerry had built : we looked in at the door, and saw the lamp burning, but we could not enter, being Christians ; they returned to tea, and the Colonel of the light horse drank two dishes of coffee made by a Gentoo servant. My master prevailed on him to sit on a chair, and they conversed together. My master told him of the works that were carrying on under his command at Bombay, which cost the Honourable Company one hundred thousand rupees per month. After tea the gentlemen played at cards, and the Gentoo Colonel left them at nine o'clock. Raggagee Angerry ordered the aide-de-camp to go and see the Colonel safe to Bombay. Next morning we set off early, and we had one of the Princes' trumpeters on horseback before us, to sound his trumpet when we were going through any town.

When we came outside the Prince's parks, we servants fell behind to stop at a publick-house. I offered to treat them with some toddy. They brought some to each of them in a cocoa-nut, for each caste. The landlady did not offer me, at first; but was prevailed upon, at last, to bring some arrack in a cocoa-nut shell. All this day's journey was near the sea-side in the Prince's country. In the evening we came to Abdalla, belonging to the Prince, where we had everything at the Prince's expense. Next morning the vessel arrived to take us over to Bombay. The trumpeter was sent back to Cowrie, and we all got on board and arrived safe at Bombay that day. His friends were glad to see him return, and the Doctor recommended him to live at his country house, Randal Lodge, on Malabar Hill, for the benefit of the air, and to use the bark; and accordingly he did so. His friends came to see him in the country. He went to town to do business; and when he had a large company he received them in his town-house; so I remained in the country, and Baba had the command in town. I always had one of the cooks and Tobie to stay with me when the Colonel was in town. At the country-house there was a Tindall that had the care of the house, slept there, and had a Gentoo girl that lived with him and passed for his wife. She desired the favour of me to give her an old shirt; and I gave two one day. All the men were in town; and the girl and her niece were asleep in the verandah, at the window of my room. I gave her a shirt, and she made my bed, and was afterwards very handy; and I gave the Tindall and her a little arrack now and then.

One night the Colonel came home late. I put him

to bed, and walked into the verandah, where all the servants were asleep in different places. The verandah is like a shade in England, to keep off the rain and the sun, where the gentlemen sit in the daytime and enjoy the air. I lay down on the Gentoo girl's left side ; and, putting my hand on her, waked and surprised her much. In a moment she put her hand to my head, and discovered, from my hair being cued, who it was. I would not intrude ; but I went to bed. Next day I told her she should not lie so near the other people ; so she sent her niece home, and laid the mat very near the window of my room. I thought it was not so hot where they lay as in the room, so I lay sometime in the verandah ; and then I put black things on that I might not be discovered. Rosilla told me, if I lay so near her again, she would tell the Tindall. I asked her, several times, to eat with me when the Tindall was present, but she would not. "People of our caste cannot eat any food dressed for a Christian, nor have any connection with those out of our own caste."

I am going to give my readers a small account of the island of Bombay. It is about fourteen miles long ; the town of the same name being at one end of the island, where all the shipping and all the business is carried on. At the other end is the town of Mayam, where there is a fortification.

In the middle of the island is the Governor's house, Parella, Malabar Hill, where was my master's, Colonel

Egerton's, Mr Hunter's, Mr Jervice's, and some
others. It is like Shooter's Hill, in Kent, but rather
higher. At the one end is a Chockee, where there
is always a European officer, having the command, on
guard. When any ships appear in sight, a signal is
made to the Castle at Bombay.

About a mile from the guard-room is a village
of the Gentoos, where is a pagoda and a grove. The
hill is mostly covered with large trees, and is hardly
known by the Europeans, except a few that live in the
island. Here the Gentoos go through all the forms of
their religion without interruption ; and their gods are
to be seen in proper form, as I mentioned of Darygan.
And all the Gentoos, when they die, are burned on
the island of Bombay, next day, by the seaside, and
the ashes of the body are cast into the sea. When a
husband dies, his wife is sometimes burned, by her
own consent and choice, with the dead husband. If
he has two wives, the first has a right to burn ; and if
she does not like it the second acquires it. Sometimes,
if the first wife has no children and the second has
children by her husband, the first wife gives the right of
being burned up to the second. If the mother does
not burn with her husband, her children live in
disgrace. They are as glad to burn as two women
in England would be to get an estate ; for they think
that they go to Heaven directly when they burn
with their husbands. But these observations are con-
fined to people of the first rank.

EIGHTEENTH-CENTURY FOOTMAN

When a woman has been married for years and has no children, and the husband is desirous to have an heir, the prieſts ask her husband if he will let her come and live in the holy place, amongſt their pagodas, for one month or six weeks, to try whether, by her own faſting and their prayers, they can prevail with their Creator that she may have a child. If he lets her come, she is taken good care of by the prieſts ; and, as her husband, who never sees her all the while, waits an answer at the end of the time mentioned, if she tells the prieſts that she is with child he is desired to come into an apartment in the pagoda, where is one of their gods cut out of ſtone, the back towards the wall and the head of pumice ſtone, hollow, with a pipe to convey water from the prieſt's room ; he is to put a fine handkerchief on the head of the idol, and continue there one hour, and then to take off his handkerchief ; if he finds it wet, it is an answer that he is to have a child. A Gentoo is only allowed two wives, but as many women as he can maintain. When a wife dies, he does not burn, but marries another. The manner of the women burning themselves with their dead husbands is as follows : A large pile of dry wood is made, and an arbour round it. The woman is dressed in her beſt clothes and jewels. Her relations and friends walk about the place conversing ; and numbers come to see the ceremony. At laſt she lays aside her jewels, and gives them her family ; she takes leave of her children and of all her friends, and is seated on the pile, having the body of her husband

laid on her lap. She speaks to him for some time in
a low voice; she then drinks a strong narcotic potion,
lights the wood, and the door is fixed. The music
sounds and the drums make a great noise, and drown
her cries. After all is reduced to ashes, the spectators
depart like people in England from a funeral. I said
to myself: " Why should I think this woman has
done wrong? She had done this to obtain Heaven
and God's favour; and have not the great and most
learned men in England and other Christian countries
done the same to gain Heaven and God's favour, who
had the Bible to direct them?" The Hindoos or
Gentoos have no Sundays, but many holidays; nor
any people in the world but Christians and Jews. I
shall say very little of the Mahomedans; they are
directed by their *Alcoran* as we are by our Bible, and
they bury in the same manner.

I shall now give a little account of the Persian
worship of fire in Bombay. About half a mile from
the Gentoos pagoda, on the highest part of Malabar
Hill, stands the Persian burying-place—a large round
tower, built of stone and lime, with an iron door.
Dogs are kept to give the alarm. No person but the
priests is allowed admittance. The fire burns in their
church night and day; and, if the house were on fire
they would not extinguish it, but run for the English.
The Persians address the fire, when they cook their
victuals; they will not even breathe on the fire, but
put a cloth over their mouths; and you cannot

disoblige them more than by throwing water on the fire. They will not blow out a candle with their breath but they will with the wind of their hand. When I lived with Colonel Dow, the Persian servant, when he went to bed at the hot wells, brought the candle for me to put out. When we walked together, I have stopped till they prayed to the sun in the east. When their women are in labour, a person in the next room could not hear them, nor suspect their situation. They bring forth their children on the bedstead, with nothing else under them. Their manner of burying is this : they follow the corpse to Malabar Hill, four miles distant, all fastened one to another and dressed in white. If one of them breaks wind, and the others smell the stink, the man is obliged to sit down on that place of the road, and never stir till the company return from the burying-place ; nor must he pray till they return. When they come to the burying place, the dead is taken in naked at the iron door. After they have gone through their prayers, they call in a dog to smell the corpse. If the dog wag his tail and seem pleased, the company lay the dead person on his back, with his face towards the sun ; for they think he was a good man. But if the dog drop his tail and turn away afraid, they think he has been a wicked man, and so they throw him down amongst the bones headlong, and return home. The birds-of-prey, which are always lurking near a Persian burying-place, hover and prey upon the carcase.

Now I return to my master. When he was at the hot wells, he had some enemies in the Council, who, taking advantage of his absence, examined his work at Bombay, and made a wrong report to the Governor. The Colonel was displeased and the dispute ran very high; and he insisted on returning to London and laying his complaint before the Directors of the Honourable East India Company. This, in a great measure, hurt his temper, and he was preparing to go with the first ship for England. One morning, when I was dressing him at the country-house, he said: " John, whether would you rather go to England with me, or remain in Bombay ? " I freely answered: " Sir, I will go to any part of the world with you." " Very well. Then you must come to the house in town, and take care of my things ; for, when the black servants hear I am going, they will begin to steal from me." " Sir, I will come, and take great care." So I took my leave of Rosilla, and Randal Lodge, and came to town. Next morning, General Wedderburne, the Commander-in-Chief, sent for our coachman, Thomas Smith, to live with him. He was an Englishman, and the only white coachman in the island ; he was a drum-major, so the General had a right to command him— which made the Colonel very angry. Soon after this, my master desired to see his clothes, and he put them in different lots. When he had put them properly together, he called me, and said: " John, pack up these clothes for me to wear in Europe ; and those others I shall give to such and such persons, and

a few things that lie on the floor, of very little value—
you may take them." "Sir", replied I, "if I remember right, you said I should have your old clothes; I
did not think you would use me like a boy." "So
you don't choose to take those things?" "Yes,
sir, I will." "I see, John, you and I will not agree
together, so provide yourself." "Sir", I replied, "I
thought I might speak what I have said." "I see we
cannot, John, so provide yourself with a master, and
you shall go this day." I said: "Very well, sir."
He desired me to make out my bill, and he discharged
me before dinner. The black men were extremely
sorry to see me turned off. Bapu said: "Is it possible,
Mr John, you are going away?" Captain Macneal
said: "John, where are you going?" "Sir, I am
going to seek a place for myself." So I left the
Colonel in 1772, after living with him fifteen months
as well as a king; and during that time I had as much
pleasure as ever a man had.

So I went to lodge in the house of a serjeant who
had married a black woman. In one week I was sent
for by Mr Shaw, a Gentleman of the Council and a
great enemy of the Colonel's. I was hired at the
town-house, and went to the country-house at Omercurry, a mile from town. Here was a great show;
for I had my liquor served me out by a Gentoo purvow.
Then I thought of the dream I had the night before I
left the Colonel. I dreamed I fell out of my bed
over a high rock, and could not get up till I went

round a large mountain. Here was a large family of servants in the kitchen, two Portuguese cooks, and five slave boys; but none of the servants had any liquor but myself, and that was very little. I drank nothing but arrack, but what I wanted I bought for myself. Mr Shaw had a public night every week, with a supper; and very often on that night a ball, besides dinners to his friends who came on business. I was confined to Omercurry with the fever and ague every three days. I went to Dr Tennant for the bark. He told me I had got the Colonel's disorder, and the best I could do would be to go to Europe. I waited to see if I could get better, but rather grew worse; and I had a great desire to go to England. There was only one Captain, a Mr Rice, to sail. I went one morning to call for him, to know if he would give me my passage to England. The Colonel came out of the dining-room first into the verandah, and said: " Well, John, are you tired of your new place already ? " " No, sir, but I am taken with the fever and the ague, and I want to go home." I took no further notice of the Colonel. When Captain Rice saw that, he came out, and I made a bow to him, with my hat in my hand. " Sir, I am come to desire the favour that you would let me have my passage to England, as I am taken with the ague, and I will pay what you desire." He told me he had not room, if I were to give him an hundred guineas. " You must wait till the first ship that sails after me." When I came downstairs, Sheek and Baba said: " Master John, you have done wrong; if you had paid the compliment to the Colonel, and desired him to have spoke to Captain Rice for you, he would have got your passage ; but they find you bear anger." I said : " I am sorry. I have neither craft nor cunning to dissemble." I went home, and remained till another opportunity. I had no work to do but to order. In the house was one Ruſtam, a Persian, who had been Steward many years, and was very rich. He was above waiting at table. He bought everything ; and, when I wanted anything, I told him, and he sent his servant ; for he kept one for himself and paid his wages. Mr Shaw would sooner lay out a guinea for anything than he would five shillings for liquor ; so Ruſtam bought for the table, and I made the bill of fare. The Moormen said : " Mr John, we like you, because God has given you a temper like a girl ; and we can do everything that we see you do, except to order a dinner or large supper. We see in Bombay, that everything is formed in your head before it is dressed, and where to put every man to his place." About two fields from Omercurry was Sally Percival's country-house. She took a walk sometimes to see me. When she wanted a letter wrote to any diſtance, she employed me. She was very fond of walking to our house, with her son in her hand. Omercurry was very pleasant : there were a great many large trees about the house and fine gardens. My maſter was generally in town all day, except when he had company. When I went to write a letter for Sally Percival, I always dined with her ; and the time was somewhat pleasant. Except when the fit of the ague and fever came on, I was pretty well. When she called for me, if I was not at home, she desired them to let Mr Shaw's writer know she wanted to speak to him. She was a good-natured and good-tempered woman as ever lived, and had not the least pride, though she was worth upwards of four thousand pounds sterling. Sometimes she conversed with me about girls who had been in keeping by gentlemen. She said: " Mr John; there are two roads, a good and an evil one. If I should step into the good one, I should like to remain there." I said: " What you say, is right, Mrs Percival, and upon my word, Madam, I believe, if you were married, you would make as good a wife as any in Asia, and, if I was good enough for you, I would propose myself for your husband." " O, do not say it, Mr John ; you are very good : if I like a man, if he had not one rupee, I would sooner have him than one with two thousand rupees with a deceitful heart. All the gentlemen here speak very well of you, Mr John."

Before the Colonel sailed, my master had said some words disrespectful of him, and the Colonel sent him a challenge. As my master was one of the Council, he made a report thereof to the Governor, and the Colonel was put under an arrest, and confined for some weeks. Captain Rice wanted to sail, as he had got his dispatches. One night after, my master was going to Mount, where Governor Hornby lived, Mr

Shaw called me, and gave me a loaded pistol and a hanger, and he took the other pistol and his sword, and said : " John, come along with me." When we came before the gate, my master said : " John, stop there till I go in and speak to Governor Hornby." When my master was in the house, one of the aide-de-camps, Captain Stuart, just alighted from his horse. When Captain Stuart saw me, it being darkish, he said : " Is this you, John ? " " Yes, sir." " Good God ! what are you doing in this warlike manner ? " " Sir, I am here with Mr Shaw, my master." " Is he with Governor Hornby ? " " Yes, sir." So it soon got wing, and went through the whole island, that Mr Shaw took John for fear of meeting with Colonel Keating, and it afforded a laugh at many a table. " Be ready, John, that is the Colonel." " Sir, I am ready ; it is only a bush, sir " ; but I declare I thought the Colonel was before us. " Are you sure, John, your pistols are primed and flints good ? " " Yes, sir."

Captain Rice sailed, and Colonel Keating with him. I remained till Captain Thomas Taylor of the *Hampshire* Indiaman arrived. As he visited at my master's house, I asked him if he would give me a passage to England. He said : " By all means ; get yourself ready, and when I sail for Europe, you shall go along with me."

At this time I had the third-day ague. When the *Hampshire* laid at Bombay, Seedy, a sovereign Prince (whom I mentioned before), came to negotiate business with the Governor and Council. He had a house made ready for him and plenty of provision for himself and all his train. When he had transacted his business, he visited all the principal men in Bombay, and wherever he came he drank some coffee made by one of his own caste.

Soon after Seedy, the Prince, went away, the Nabob of Broach came on business with the Governor and Council; he had four hundred and fifty men in his train. The house allotted for the Nabob was joining my master's town house, and his tents were pitched before our house, and Governor Hornby allowed the Nabob's standard to be set up at the head of his little camp. He continued at Bombay three weeks; his attendants were very richly dressed; he had two bands of music, which played all the night when he was asleep; the one relieved the other.

When his affairs were settled, the Nabob visited the Governor and all the Council at their houses, and General Wedderburne at his country-house, where he went on a visit. He had two hundred men to attend him, mostly in arms, with colours flying.

When he came to see my master at Omercurry, he entered our parlour, sat down with our master, and conversed. All his principal servants entered and

168

ſtood round the whole time, and I behind my maſter's chair.

It is thought a grand thing in Asia to have an European servant. As the Nabob was a Mahomedan, our two servants, of his caſte, served him with coffee, and the rose-water sprinkled on the parlour. This was all the entertainment he had, where he visited. He ate at home, and his victuals were dressed by his own cook.

The *Hampshire* only waited for a fair wind. The passengers were all ordered on board. I took my leave of Bombay, and went on board, and then the ague and fever left me. I waited at the Captain's table, as there were a good many passengers, and I messed with the Captain's servants. I got better every day.

The firſt place we ſtopped at was Tillicherry. Mr Boddam was Chief at that time. We ſtopped ten days to take in pepper and other goods. The Captain took me on shore with his own servant, James Clerke who was a fine singer, and we enjoyed ourselves every night at an Englishman's, who kept a public-house in Tillicherry. It is one of the pleasanteſt places I ever saw. We next ſtopped at Cuchiline, which belongs to the Dutch; we ſtopped here two nights to buy provisions, which were in plenty and cheap.

When we were a month out from Bombay, we ſtopped at Anjengoe, a place of our own, to complete our loading. We were here a week; fowls sold here at the rate of eight for a rupee, and pine-apples at one penny each, and everything else in proportion. When an English soldier goes on guard, he takes two bottles of arrack to drink in the night.

When the Honourable Company's goods were all on board and the ship ready to sail, the wind blew very ſtrong; the sea was very rough, and the Captain was afraid of a lee-shore. The Captain desired his servant and me to go on board and take the other gentlemen's servants with us. We carried the Captain's and the other passenger's linens. Anjengoe was the laſt port we were to touch at in India. The *Hampshire* was two miles from shore at anchor. The Captain came to the beach to see us over the higheſt surf, the higheſt in Asia, except Madras. We got over the firſt and second, but the third was about twelve feet high. It blew so ſtrong that it threw our boat and all of us into the sea, and with a great ſtruggle we saved our lives and the articles we had.

After dinner we were sent back. Mr Reinek, the Chief, came down to the beach to see the coolies do their duty in taking us off. At this time all the things were wet, and of course more heavy; we got over the firſt and second as before, but the third overthrew us all together. The linens, being wet, went to the bottom. The next surf knocked the coolie-boat upon James Clerke, the Captain's servant, and broke his thigh.

We had a hard struggle for our lives. We came back to Mr Reinek's house, and stopped till next morning. It being calmer, we got easy off; the things were all lost. James Clerke was left behind, and when we got on board I took his place. We had a good passage for England, till we came between the latitude of the fourth part of Madagascar and the Cape of Good Hope. There we had tempestuous weather for three weeks with a foul wind, so that the Captain furled the sails and lashed up the helm, and let the ship drive where she would.

Captain Taylor and his officers were in great trouble of mind. We got so near the Cape, with a lee-shore, that we could see the tableland and the Lyon's Rump, and, had the wind continued, we should have dashed against the rocks; but it pleased God the wind changed and carried us further on the sea. We had very bad weather going round the Cape of Good Hope, insomuch that the whole ship's company expected every day to be lost. Sometimes the officers on watch were knocked down on deck by a sea coming overboard, and the men were washed overboard and never seen again. One time two men were washed over, and the next sea threw them in again. One of our best seamen was easing himself on the head, and a sea washed him away. He called out: "A rope, a rope, Captain"; but he disappeared, and was never seen afterwards.

The weather was so stormy that the sailors said they saw the Flying Dutchman. The common story is that this Dutchman came to the Cape in diſtress of weather, and wanted to get into harbour, but could not get a pilot to conduct her, and was loſt; and that ever since, in very bad weather, her vision appears. The sailors fancy that, if you would hail her, she would answer like another vessel. At length we got into the trade-winds, and had fine weather, so that we hardly shifted a sail for two weeks, when the ship's company had ease after hard work. We came down with pleasure to St Helena, and ſtopped ten days. On shore I was Acting Steward, and Captain Taylor's servant. As they dine early at St. Helena, we walked every day after dinner up the country amongſt the white farmers. As the country is very high, we could see a great way at sea; and up the country we saw a great many white girls, farmer's daughters.

St Helena is a wholesome, pleasant place, and a fine keen searching air. If noblemen and gentlemen of Great Britain and Ireland would go to Madeira and St Helena for their health, inſtead of going to France and Portugal, they would be sure to re-eſtablish their health.

When Captain Taylor had ſtopped as long as he wished for, and had got provisions and water on board, he set sail for the island of Ascension, sixteen degrees north from St Helena. The Captain ſtopped two days to get fish and turtle for the ship's company, which are got there in plenty. No person lives on the island, because there is neither water, rain, nor spring. The island has no grass all the year round. It is thirty miles round, and has very high mountains; but where the ships come to anchor it is level, and the sand on the beach is as white as snow. When an officer and his men go on shore to catch turtle, the men run and turn them on their back, while they are asleep at night on the beach. While they laſt, the whole ship's company have turtle to eat, and sometimes one ship will catch forty or fifty large ones. From Ascension we set sail, and the firſt place we ſtopped at was Portsmouth, where we were a few days ; and again we set sail, and arrived at Blackwall, after a passage of about six months, and I had been gone from England four years. I ſtopped with Captain Taylor one month till the ship was unloaded.

I was out of place three months. I hired myself to James Nowland, Esq., in Newman Street, Oxford Street. This gentleman gave Mr Shaw my chara&ter in the island of Bombay. When I left Colonel Keating I lived with him six months. One Sunday, in particular, when he had company : after dinner he called for a pack of cards, and there happened to be none in the house, and I could get none to buy. He rang the bell in anger, and because I could not get him cards to play, he turned me away. Next maſter I had, was Mr Lecall, a Dutchman, who lodged in Pall Mall Court. His Dutch servant had returned, and as I was acquainted at the house, I called there. By chance, the miſtress went upſtairs and spoke about me, and as the people of the house knew me he took me without a charaćter. I lived with him three months. Every Monday morning, he gave me fifteen shillings per week, and I had plenty of everything beside that I wanted. He had his dinners from the Star and Garter. He was as good a maſter as ever I met with. If he did not come home by twelve at night, I was to go to bed; and he came home to breakfaſt. He said: "John, I am under the necessity of going to Paris before I return to Amſterdam; you had better go with me, and I shall not have to hire a servant in Paris, as you know the city of Paris." "Sir, I will go round Cape Horn with you, if you please." So he allowed me one shilling per day more for travelling. We set out for Dover in a poſt-chaise, and crossed over to Calais, and in the same manner set off poſt for Paris. We put up at Monsieur Semunnilie's Hôtel de Park Royal, Rue Faubourg, St Germaine, at the apartments Mr Crauford had when I was with him in Paris. He found he muſt have a carriage, as there are not chairs as in London. I went to the same livery-ſtables that furnished Mr Crauford with a chaise and horses, and I desired a carriage to attend my maſter; when he said, "John, if you do not like to go out with the chariot, get a lackey's place." I told him I would go out with the carriage with all my heart, and save him that expense; and, by going out with the chariot, I have one livre per day from the master of the chariot and horses, as is the custom in Paris.

We were three months in Paris, which made ninety livres ; for my master jaunted about Paris and went to Versailles. Louis the XV was there at that time. It is a fine place, much like Windsor ; and the gardens are very large. I went to the King's fine chapel on Sunday. The King, the Dauphin and Dauphiness were in the gallery at one end of the chapel. We stopped here one week.

I can hardly express the pleasure I had with Mr Lecall. When his business was done, we went post to Lille in Flanders, and we were there two days. From thence we went to Ypres, a city belonging to the Dutch. At this place his coachman came with his chariot and horses, and stopped here one day to rest the horses. The coachman could not speak French nor English, and I could speak no Dutch ; but we spent the evening agreeably together. The landlord was interpreter between us. My master paid me, and went home ; and next day I set off, and in two days arrived at Calais and crossed over to Dover. After my arrival in London, I soon got another master to go abroad with, Mr Dawson from Dublin. We set off for the German Spa, through Flanders. My master had a great liking for this country. The people were just after his own heart; for he had a great desire for gambling, and that is the delight of foreigners

My master was gone from England one year, and in
that he gained one thousand pounds; what he lost
and gained, he marked down in a book. One night at
Lisle, coming home, he told me; "John, I have
just gained one thousand pounds". "Sir, I am very
glad; for that will clear your expenses." "Very
nearly," said he. My master and a Mr Stuart from
Holland, a Scotch gentleman, kept house together at
Spa, while he stopped at Spa. In six weeks Mr
Stuart went home. My master then got Colonel
O'Fagan, in the Emperor's service, to be in the house
with him. He had a German valet and footman.
My master went very often to Aix-la-Chapelle. At
the hôtel of Madam Buches there were always a great
many ladies and gentlemen. She had a daughter
married to a gentleman in Liége, and a pretty girl at
home unmarried. Madam Buches had her coachman
and footman in livery, and so had her son-in-law,
which made her house more respected by the ladies
and gentlemen.

My master was in this country five months, in
Aix-la-Chapelle, Spa, Liége, and Brussels; then in
the winter at Paris, where we put up at the Hôtel
de Saxe, Rue Faubourg, St Germaine. My master
got a carriage, coachman and footman, and he gave a
rich livery, and made as genteel appearance as any in
Paris. He went to Versailles, and as far as Bourdeaux
where he had relations in the wine-trade, and there
we were six weeks, and then came to London by sea.

After being in London a few weeks, we went to Holyhead, in Wales, and to Dublin in the packet. Mr Dawson's house was in the Mall. He had a large family of servants. I stopped two weeks at the house; then he got me a master, one Mr Brown, who was going to London on business. I hired myself with him two months. He lodged in the Haymarket, at the Seven Stars, a milliner's. He left London. Mr Brown and another gentleman took a post for Park Gate. I was then out of place. Soon after I heard of a gentleman wanting a servant to go into Wales. Mr Bate, at his hôtel in the Adelphi, told me to go to Mr Freeman in the Temple. When I saw him, he said: " Did Mr Bate send you to me ? " " Yes, sir." " I want a servant to go with me, as it is the vacation, and the company is out of town; to dress me; and go round the west of England; and I want to see Wales. My servant is of no use to travel, as he cannot dress hair "; so we set out in two days for Oxford, Cheltenham, Worcester, and Gloucester, and Malvern Wells. He was well pleased with the journey, and liked the prospect and situation of the house at the Wells much.

When we left Gloucestershire, going over Malvern Hills, my master, as being before, saw a long bundle on the road. He said: " John, take up that bundle and see what is in it." I got off my horse and opened the bundle, and found two new shifts, a gown, two pairs of sheets, and two pairs of stockings. " It is your property, sir, as you saw it first." My master said: " John, lay the bundle on the stone or hang it on that tree, and whoever has lost it will find it when they come to look for it." I said : " Sir, I beg your pardon, but I had rather not, but take it along with me, for another person may take it whose property it is not. Sir, I beg you will let me take it." So we went on, and by and by a boy came running along, and said : " Gentlemen, did you see a bundle we dropped it from the waggon as we came from Gloucester city ? " My master said ; " Who does the bundle belong to ? " " Please, your honour, it belongs to my young mistress ; she went with the waggon to buy the things that are in the bundle. She is going to be married next week." " What is her name ? " " Sir, her name is Molly Williams ; she is farmer Williams's daughter ; she is to be married to young Bob Giles, the cooper." My master said : " My servant has got the bundle, and when we over-take the waggon, she shall have it." When we came alongside of the waggon, my master said : " My dear, I have found your bundle, I hear you are to be married." " Yes, sir." " Take care of your bundle, otherwise it may not fall into so good hands again." " Sir, I am very much obliged to you." " I have one thing to tell you, my dear ; take great care of your maidenhead, and, if you should lose it, if you do not cry ' O ', you will never get it again."

We went to Ross, Hereford, Monmouth, Chepstow,

Abergaveny, and back to Chepſtow again. My maſter admired this place much. He said it was as sweet a rural place as ever he saw. He ſtopped two days at the Three Cranes. He desired me to have what punch I liked to drink in the evening with the farmers, which was the cause of a good deal of money being spent, and the landlord was sorry when we came away. We crossed the Old Ferry, and came to Briſtol; and next day we came to Bath and ſtopped; and at the end of eight weeks from London, he returned, after a pleasant journey. I left him, and as I was coming along Coventry Street, I met one of Mr Maines's clerks, the banker in Jermyn Street. He asked if I was in place. I said: "Sir, I have juſt left one." "John go to Mr Hill's, who lodges in Pall Mall, at No. 23. He comes out of Yorkshire, and is going to France. He gets money at our house when he wants; tell him you came from our house." Accordingly I went next morning; and being very well dressed, with a gold-laced veſt and other things in form, I went up-ſtairs. He asked me several queſtions, such as: "Did you go with these gentlemen as a servant or as a companion?" "I am a servant, sir, and not a proud one, I do assure you." "Very well; give me your address, and, if I want you, I will send for you." As I was coming out, I met a German going up. I went into the next public-house, and soon after this man came in. I asked him if he had success. He said he had, and was to go to France with him. "He spoke to me about you, and said you were more like a gentleman than a servant; now, I am plain dressed, and I have got the place." Three days after I went after Sir Francis Hobburn's place. I was dressed plain, without lace. I went upstairs to him. He was going on his travels. When he saw me, he said he had got one. When I came downstairs he rang the bell, and said to his footman: "How came you to send that fellow to me? Is he dressed like a person for my place or like an interpreter?" When he came down, he said: "I am sorry I did not tell you to dress yourself finer, for Sir Francis is very nice." After this, I was sent to Sir William Abdy's place. I went at night, and well dressed. Sir William not being at home, Lady Abdy told me she did not want a servant. Three days after I saw the servant that sent me after the place, who said: "I am sorry you went dressed in a gold-laced waistcoat. Against the candle light it made a more rich appearance. She said you were too grand for a family servant." I said to myself: "A man does not know what to do for the best in this world." The next master I had I got in an odd manner, in Brewer Street, Golden Square. I met an acquaintance of my own, who told me he had been after a place. "A young gentleman, at Mr Gordon's, an undertaker's house, was come to London for his health and the advice of the doctors. I asked a guinea a week and he would not give it; if you like, you may go and see what he will give you." I told him I would, and bid him go into the public-house till I came back. I knew that a young gentleman from the country, not accustomed to keep a servant, would not give that money. I called for Mr Lowrie at Mr Gordon's, and I was sent up to his room. " Sir, I believe you want a servant." " I do." After asking some questions, and he was pleased with the answers, he said ; " What shall I give you per week ? " " Fifteen shillings, sir, if you please." " I will give you that, so come in the morning, and there is half-a-crown to drink." I thanked him and promised to be with him in the morning. I went to my friend and told him what had happened, and treated him with half-a-crown's worth of liquor. He was like to hang himself, for not taking Mr Lowrie's kind offer. Dr Smith, a relation of his, attended my master. I lived with him near half a year. The doctor was very well pleased with my attention to my master ; I was his nurse and cook, and made all his drinks ; it was a good place for me as ever a man could wish to enjoy. I had several presents for my attention.

My master got well and went into Scotland ; then I was out of place some months, and lived on the fruits of my labour : that was my custom ; when in place I was careful, and out of place I went genteel and was sober, and was ready in three hours to go anywhere in the world. Next place I had was to live with George Spencer, Esq., Norfolk Street, in the Strand. I hired myself to him for forty guineas per year ; he was a Madeira merchant and had his partners in Madeira. He commonly lived in Norfolk Street ; but he went

into the country through the West of England, and
he stopped in Bath and Bristol weeks at a time : he was
mostly on the move ; he delighted in travelling.
When on the road, he never had a bottle of wine but
I had part of it. He went to see his friends in Dublin
the Madeira Merchants ; and it was the only place in
the world I liked to go to. I saw my old acquaintance.
I gave a ball to all my friends, at a public-house in
Chapel Street to upwards of forty people. That it
might be no trouble to the landlord, I had one ham
baked, and three turkeys cold put into a sideroom to eat
when they liked. I gave punch, wine, and negus, and
whatever the house afforded. The company were all
gone by two in the morning, being mostly gentlemen's
servants, men, and maids. When they were gone
I drank a bottle of wine with the landlord. I had
liberty the whole night. I paid my bill, four pound
ten shillings ; the music, fifteen shillings, and five
shillings to the two servants for their trouble ; in all
five pounds ten shillings. There was neither glass nor
plate broke, the company behaved so well. At this
time I was called the "Handsome Macdonald".
If I called for any person, if they were out, the maid
would tell, when her fellow-servant came home :
"Mr Macdonald called." "Which Mr Macdonald ?"
—for in Dublin there were a great many of that name—
the maid would say it was the "Handsome Macdonald" that gave the ball. In London I was called
"Beau Macdonald" by the men and "The Scotch
Frenchman".

We had great pleasure in this jaunt to Ireland. My master went first to the city of Cork to settle his bills with the wine-merchants, and then returned to Dublin, and afterwards to Belfast in the north of Ireland. We travelled in a noddy from Dublin and back again, that is, a one-horse chaise, and the driver sits behind the horse, so the horse draws three people. On the north road I could give my master a description of the country, as I had been there before. We returned to Dublin, and then through Wales to London. I lived with my master one year. One day in particular my master dined out, and I waited on him, and at night we both came home merry; when I put his hair in papers, and undressed him, I took up his shoes in my left hand, and put his coat over the same arm; and seeing me do so he said: "You take up my clothes as if you had never seen any clothes before." "Sir, I have handled better than yours many times." He turned me out of the room and next morning he discharged me; so I lost a good place for speaking one foolish word, and I was very sorry for it.

In two weeks after, I was walking through St James's Park, and I met James Macpherson, Esq. of Manchester Buildings. He asked me if I was in place. I told him I had left George Spencer, Esq. about two weeks ago, and got no master at present. He said he was going to France, and would take me along with him. "Come in the morning; I shall go to Dover to-morrow night, my black man will pack up my clothes." I went in the morning, and we set out in a poſt-chaise to Dover that night, and next day crossed over to Calais, and slept there that night. Next day we set off for Paris, and put up at the Hôtel d'Angleterre, Rue Rukelow, and there my maſter was two months. He had a carriage, coachman, and footman. My maſter and some other gentlemen in company went to Versailles for one day. The palace is handsome, the gardens extensive, and the ſtables the handsomeſt I ever saw in my life. At this time Louis XV was ill of the smallpox, and died while we were in France. When my maſter left Paris, he went poſt to Lille, afterwards to Ypres. We ſtopped in this city one week. The three Scotch regiments lay here, called the Scotch Hollanders; they were commanded by Colonels Stuart, Gordon, and Johnſtone. I thought myself in Scotland, seeing so many of my own countrymen.

When we left Ypres, we went to Dunkirk, and through Graveline to Calais; we were here two days and then crossed over to Dover, then home to London. As I was only with my maſter for the journey, I was paid next day; and again I was out of place. The next maſter I had was James Coutts, Esq., banker, in the Strand, who was going to make the tour of England for his health. He waited one month in London before he could get a servant to dress him. He wore a wig over his hair. He had twenty servants that came, but they could not dress him. It required a person that underſtood the business of wig-making. When he was dressed, no person could tell there was anything but his own hair ; and he had the handsomeſt head and face I ever saw in my life. He hired me and next day we set out for his country-house, at Hampton Village, then for Cheltenham with our coach and four horses, and two saddle-horses. My maſter was accompanied by his daughter, Miss Coutts and her cousin Miss Stuart, of Allan Bank, in Scotland. There were the coachman and poſtilion, the footboy and I. When on the road, the first thing I did in the morning was to knock at the ladies' door to call them. At other times they got up when they pleased. At this time there was at Cheltenham a great deal of company. My maſter lodged at a Quaker's house the proprietor of the Wells. We went out every day airing. It is the cuſtom at the Wells to go out after breakfaſt and after dinner. We went to Malvern Wells, and to the city of Glouceſter, a night at one place, and a night at the other place, and back to Cheltenham again. We ſtopped at Cheltenham two months, and jaunting about in this manner. Then we set off for Worceſter, Birmingham, Mancheſter, Preſton, Matlock Wells, and called at all the noblemen and gentlemen's houses on the road, and so on in this manner to Carlisle city. We travelled to every part worth seing in the north of England. We crossed the Tweed from Cornhill to Coldſtream, and remained in that beautiful country, the south part of Scotland, two months, visiting from one family to another; but we were chiefly in the Merse, at the house of Sir John Stuart of Allan Bank, my master's cousin. We went to Kelso, Berwick, Dunse, and went over to the Holy Island a few days; and we partook of several kettles of fish on the banks of the Tweed, which merry feats are always accompanied with dancing. When we left this place, we went to Harrogate. From thence we went to London and afterwards to my master's house at Hampton. After he had been at home some time, my master found he must go somewhere else; and his physicians advised him to go to Italy for the air of that country, and he consented; therefore I had warning given me, as he was obliged to have an Italian servant to take my place. Mr Rosi was hired, but did not come home till my master was ready to go.

Mr Coutts was so well pleased with my service for seven months, as I never was once out of the way, made all sorts of drinks that was ordered for him, and whatever he wanted, that he made me several presents of clothes; and, when he paid me my wages, he gave me two guineas over, and told Mr Brown, the wine-merchant in Craven Street, to recommend me.

I went to Dover with Mr Coutts, and returned when he and the ladies went on board of ship. I came back to London, and in two weeks Sir John Stuart, of Allan Bank, came to London on his way to Portugal, for the benefit of his health. I suppose I had been recommended for his servant, when he should come to London, by Mr. Coutts. He called for me at two or three places. I heard of it. I went to him at Mrs Elliot's, in Brewer Street, where he lodged. He told me he was going to Lisbon for his health; that he did not think he should live till he reached there; and, if I was not engaged, he would take me with him. I told him I should be very happy to embrace the offer. He had a carriage, and ſtopped a few weeks in London, and in winter, November, 1776, we set out for Salisbury. Sir John was then twenty years of age: then for Dorcheſter; after to Exeter; there my maſter was one week waiting for Mr March, a gentleman going to Lisbon, of his acquaintance. When Mr March came, we went poſt to Falmouth, and we ſtopped there near a week till a fair wind came round. We went on board the *Expedition* packet, Captain Robertson, with a great many passengers, ladies and gentlemen, many who had never been at sea before. We set sail with a fair wind. The weather was fine for that time of the year, but the fine day caused a great confusion at night. The ship not being prepared for a ſtorm, the tarpaulin not being over the hatchways and other places open, a great ſtorm arose in the middle of the night. When we got in the Bay of Biscay, all at once all hands were called to save the sails and maſts. The hatchways being uncovered, we shipped a sea, which made the whole ship's company think we were going to the bottom. In a moment much water came in as set the chests a-floating. In three minutes more, we shipped another, which knocked me out of my hammock. Then I believe we all said : "God have mercy on us !" I laid in one of the men's hammocks in the galley, on the lee-side ; of course on the lower side, for the ship was near on her broadside before the sails were lowered. The chests and trunks rolled on me, I could hardly get out : I crawled out with great difficulty, and went into the cuddy where the Captain and the gentlemen dined. My master was there in his hammock. When he saw me, he said : "Good God, John, I suppose we shall all be lost, what shall I do ? Must I get up ?" "Sir, do you lie still ; there is no danger, we have got a land wind." "What is a land wind ?" "Sir, a wind that comes from the land that will drive us out to sea, and then there is no danger when we have got sea-room." I sat and kept hold of the mast, just beside my master. By this time the ladies and gentlemen were in fits. When the sails and masts were saved, the hatches were covered over. It rained, and the wind was wonderfully strong ; but as God would have it, no lives were lost. The Captain and most of the ship's company had their wives and families at Falmouth, and there was such crying for fear of never seeing them again. One of the mariners that had been in the trade for eighteen years was frightened into fits. After the greatest danger was over, the Captain lay down ; he got up again light-headed. Sir John asked me if I did not think it best for him to get up. " No, sir, you are in the beſt place you can be ; for there is not the leaſt danger. Do not show the leaſt marks of fear, and then they cannot laugh at you. The ladies have been in fits and some of the gentlemen also. For my part, I have been in worse ſtorms than this many times ; and, had the ship been prepared, we should not have been so ill off as we are." We waited with patience till seven in the morning, when I got my maſter up to clear the place for breakfaſt. By this time he was glad he took my advice to lay ſtill in the night. Finding things were out of danger, my maſter went on deck, where he saw such a scene as he never saw before ; the sea was very high indeed and the wind continued so my maſter ſtood for one hour, without ſtirring, to see the raging of the sea, and the mariners putting things to rights after the night's fright.

Mr March and my maſter were speaking about the ſtorm. He said : " Sir John, this lets you know what the poor mariners go through in a hurricane, and in a battle at sea." The rough weather continued, so that my maſter wore one shirt for ten days. After this we had fine weather, and kept our Chriſtmas on sea, and the company was very happy ; but one fine moonlight night we saw a man-of war making after us, full sail, and put up all the sail we could ; but she gained on us, and the Captain made the ship ready to fight. The mail was brought up to be ready to throw overboard. They fired some guns after us to bring us to. Mr Bowen, a gentleman of Falmouth went on the poop, and I ſtood with him. He said we were as safe there as below. The man-of-war was ſtill gaining on us, but the Captain put off no time to make ready. By and by, two Portuguese gentlemen came up to look how things were going on ; and that moment a ball came across our ship's rigging. They both went down directly to the passengers and told this. So you may consider our situation. We thought they would be all taken. Soon after, another ball came across our fore-ship ; and they hailed us, and desired our Captain to lay to ; and so he did : and after all, we found her to be our friend—the ship was the *Earl of Dunmore*. The Captain of the *Dunmore* let our Captain know he would send one of his officers on board of us to hear the news, for he had been a great while from England. By and by this officer and boat's crew came to us as bold as heroes. I said to myself: " I will be damned but you have a great ſtock of impudence to put our gentlemen and ladies in such a fear." By this time the passengers were come up to the Captain's dining-place. When the Captain received the Lieutenant of the man-of-war, he entered so bold that the ladies looked at him with fear, surprise and gladness, the same as the daughters of king Darius did at Alexander when he took them in their tents. He received the news, and informed us of what he knew. He drank grog ; and his men had grog to drink alongside. So they went away again, and the passengers went to bed with easy minds. For two days more we had a pleasant passage, and got in sight of the rock of Lisbon. When we came near the entrance of the river, a poor fisherman came on board and took the command of the ship to pilot her into the Tagus to the anchoring-place, on the laſt night of the year. We all went to the English hôtel, kept by Mr and Mrs Dewar from Northumberland. Next morning, at breakfaſt, we laughed to think we had been in Lisbon part of two years. The hôtel was large, and ſtood on the higheſt ground near Lisbon, neareſt the sea. There was a great deal of company in the hôtel, English, Irish, Scots, Welsh, gentlemen and servants. Some had carriages, others horses, while they remained at Lisbon ; and they made a fine appearance when they went together an airing. Sir John had a carriage and coachman and two saddle-horses. The owner of the saddle-horses was an Englishman, and he aſted as footman and groom. My maſter made the genteeleſt appearance of any gentleman in Lisbon. As my maſter and I were going into Spain, at our departure from Lisbon, we both had a Spanish maſter. We did not mind the Portuguese language. My maſter made not any improvement in the Spanish language, he was so much out. But I ſtopped at home, and got my lesson when the other servants went out amongſt whores and after their own fun ; and they laughed at me for ſtaying at home ; but, by and by, when their doſtor's bills came in, I laughed at them. After eight weeks at Lisbon, when we were on the road, they were obliged to call me to interpret for them. When they left Lisbon their pleasure there was over, and I enjoyed my own satisfaction. My master, though he could speak French and Latin as well as English, was obliged to ask me the names of things in Spanish because, when I was in Lisbon, I lost no time, but learned as much of the Spanish language as I could.

Lisbon is the finest situation of a city in the world for trade and a fine air. It is built on seven hills, on the side of a fine river. You may see fifty miles across a fine country by looking out of the windows in Lisbon. The river is eight miles broad just against the city. If you are a mile on the river in a boat you may see every house in town at one view. At this time General Maclean, a Scotsman, was Commander-in-Chief of the army in Portugal. I have often thought he had more respect paid to him than the Royal family had to them. Soon after we arrived in Lisbon, a princess died six weeks old. She had a grander burial than a king or queen.

People of age go into purgatory to suffer for their sins, till they are prayed out of purgatory; but as she had committed no sin, she was to be received into Heaven directly. At the funeral there were about fifteen hundred horse in the procession, carrying noblemen and gentlemen; besides carriages most grandly dressed with caps and feathers. In a few days after the King was taken ill, and kept his bed a long time, till all his physicians gave him over. They told the Queen they could prescribe no more for him. She was the King of Spain's own sister. She desired to call Dr Wade that attended the English in Lisbon. He was an Irish gentleman. He was desired to see the King next morning. The Queen said to the physicians: " What shall we do that the King may not be alarmed by seeing a new face ? " They answered the Queen they would ſtand round the King's bed as usual ; and that Dr Wade should look through under one of our arms. It was agreed to by the Queen. When the Doctor saw the Queen, after seeing the King, he told her he would give the King what would be of service to him. So he saw the King every morning in the same manner as I have mentioned. He had the King six weeks under his care, which was the time he lived. Dr Wade was rewarded for his skill, and he was also knighted ; his name was now Sir John Wade, and he lived very much respected ; and, when he was sent for by the Portuguese, he had double the fees they gave their own countrymen. Sir John, my maſter jaunted round the country, and was got a great deal better, and began to think of going overland to Cadiz, in Spain. He hired a chaise and mules, and mules for the baggage ; and he had an interpreter to go as far as the confines of Portugal. There were two French gentlemen in company with my maſter, going to Cadiz ; they had a chaise and black servant. After dinner we sailed across the river Tagus, where our chaises were ready at the inns at Aldea Gallega, at the sign of the Frog ; there we were shown up to a very long room with nothing in it, but in ten minutes I furnished the place. Henry, the interpreter, and I put up our camp, table, ſtools, my maſter's camp bed, and Miss Kitty's curtains. I opened up my little case with wine, and put it on the table for Sir John. We had one end of the room and the two Frenchmen the other. I put out the travelling-pye, and the gentlemen had another. We had plates and dishes made of tin, knives, spoons, glasses, pepper, our own candles, everything for our use. As it was early in the night for supper, my maſter asked me if I could get him a dish of the Queen of Scots soup. I sent Henry to inquire if he could get chickens, eggs, and parsley below. I made a fine dish of soup, and Sir John invited the Frenchmen to sup with him. They liked the soup, and ate nothing else. No person belonging to the house came near us; and we wanted nothing below but water, and a kettle to boil the soup. When I was in the kitchen, I had an opportunity of seeing the family go to supper. The maſter, miſtress, children, and maid sat down as if they feared God. He took off his hat, put it before his face, and said grace. We all slept in one room: Henry and I had only one blanket, and our great coats under our heads.

From the time I left Lisbon till I returned to England, I became, or travelled, as a Roman Catholic. I have seen many different religions, and found it was beſt to pay respeĉts to the people and conform to their religion. In the morning we packed up our baggage, and paid our bills. The two chaises brought to the door two mules for Henry and me; a man on foot to bring our two mules back, and another man with two mules, for our baggage. Each of us wore a sword or hanger. We never went faster than a waggon in England, except downhill. The carriages are strong and heavy laden. The roads are bad in the spring.

When my master saw that the two gentlemen had only one chaise for them and their black boy, he desired one of them to come in with him; so we set off for Pamella through a fine country. One of the Frenchmen gave me his gunpowder and shot and net that I might shoot game as I rode along. I put the powder, shot and bag for the game round my shoulder, and the gun in my hand; and was glad of the opportunity, as it is an open country and the game plenty. I had great luck. I rode on a little before, and I often shot the game in view of the gentlemen. My mule stopped in a moment, and neither of the mules were afraid of the report of the gun. What I shot in the day Henry and I dressed at night.

We got to Pamella by noon—a fine village. We dined there. After stopping long enough to refresh, we set off for St Ubes, a large town. In the morning we went for Molines, and on our way crossed the river Cadaon. After dinner we went through a fine level country, between two ridges of fine high hills, and at night arrived at Alcaar, where we stopped. We were obligated to go and buy anything we wanted. The maid supplied us in the kitchen with wood and water, and Henry and I were cooks. In the morning we left Alcaar to go to Gandola. This day we crossed two branches of the river Cadaon, and the same day we bought twenty-four full-grown sweet oranges for threepence, it being a fine country for fruit and trees. On our right, to the weſt of Gandola, was a large ridge of mountains covered with trees, and the country well cultivated. After dinner we passed through Villa, and through Terrier Adaves, both on branches of the river Guadiana, one of the longeſt rivers in all Spain. In the morning of this day one of the French gentlemen asked Henry to come into the chaise with the black boy, and let him ride his mule. Henry went into the chaise, and the gentleman rode along with me. We both conversed on different things. It was a fine day, and I had plenty of sport with the gun. At laſt I came to a cross road, where was the Virgin Mary, and Chriſt in her arms. I put off my hat, lowered it, and put it on again, and then crossed myself. He said : "Don't you belong to the Church of England " ? "Yes, sir." "I thought you never paid any reſpeſt, in your worship, to the holy Virgin." "In our worship we do not, but we eſteem her."

At night we came to a fine large city called Bijah, with fine houses and well fortified. Here we had very good inns. The gentlemen had a bed, and so had Henry and I ; but Sir John lay in his own bed. We had fish, partridges, and chickens, with vegetables; and we had fine wine and everything agreeable. Opposite to the inn was a ball of the middling sort of the young people in town. After my master was gone to bed, Henry and I went over, and we were let in. We sat and saw them dance country-dances, and dance in the Portuguese manner, which was very entertaining. I paid a quarter dollar for Henry and me, and came away. They were very civil to us: but there was nothing at the ball to drink. When the young gentlemen handed the girls to their chairs after the dance was done, they took their snuff-box out of their pocket, and gave their partner a pinch of snuff. We came home and had some wine to drink, and left them to take snuff.

In the morning early we set off for Mortola, on the confines of Portugal. This day we passed through the most beautiful country for hills, woods, and waters. We crossed several branches of the river Guadiana. We passed through Alvistil, a fine town, Massejena, another fine large town; and dined at Alcarina. After dinner we passed through some villages, and passed by some convents; and in the evening arrived at Mortola. This town stands very high on the banks of the river Guadiana, surrounded by a great number of very high hills of bare rocks, more barren and wild than ever I saw in the Highlands of Scotland. We put up at the only inn in town, a very good one. The master and mistress were very good people; we had plenty of every thing. I made the Queen of Scots soup, and the mistress and I drank a bottle of wine together. There was something singular in the man that walked along with us to bring back the two saddle-mules. He was one of the most obliging and condescending men I ever saw. You could not speak to him but off went his hat. He was always alongside my mule. When I gave him a penny to get a pint of wine he was as happy as a prince.

Here we discharged our chaises and mules, because we were to go by water. We were very good customers to the house. Besides what we had in the house, we had provisions from them to serve us on the water.

Next day, after breakfast, we all went into a boat to go down the river for Agomenta, in Spain. We sailed ten miles on the river in Portugal, and twenty between Portugal and Spain ; Portugal on our right hand and Spain on our left. Sometimes we went ashore in Spain ; at other times in Portugal, at the villages. In the evening we came to Castromarin, a fine new village. Here we remained till Sir John showed the Governor of Javira his passport and got another to go out of Portugal. I must say of the country people, they are civil, innocent, and harmless ; though it is said a man's life is in danger, in Lisbon, if he be out late at night. That may be because the desperate, in all countries, flock to the capital.

EIGHTEENTH-CENTURY FOOTMAN

The Portuguese at a diſtance from Lisbon are as much afraid of the Lisbonites as any other ſtrangers. My maſter was not ready till the afternoon of the next day. Then we crossed the river, and went in to the city of Agamonte in Spain. We left the two French gentlemen behind at Caſtromarin; the river, at this part, is three miles broad. Sir John was shown to the beſt inns in town. We had good wine and a good supper, made ready by the landlady, a widow, a good sort of a woman. When the cloth was laid, they put three covers on the table. But, when I put down the supper, I took off all the plates but one, and I waited on my maſter; and when he was done, Henry and I supped very comfortably in the same room, for it was both parlour and kitchen.

When we crossed the river from Portugal to the city of Agamonte we entered into the province of Andalusia, formerly a kingdom. In the morning the gentleman that my maſter was recommended to sent for a man, and hired five mules to carry us and the baggage. This gentleman, Mr Lepo, lent Sir John an English saddle to be returned with the mules. Henry and I rode above the baggage. When all was ready, we rode through the fine city of Agamonte. As we were riding along the ſtreet, a fine woman came to look out of the window; but, seeing us, she in a moment disappeared, for fear that anyone should see her looking after ſtrangers. Agamonte is a fine city for trade, being near the sea, on the banks of the river, in a fine cultivated country. We went to Taron to dinner; and, at night, to Lepe, through a beautiful level country. All this day's journey was near the sea. Taron and Lepe are fine large towns; but no women to be seen. The Spaniards, like the Portuguese, are kind and civil; and have not the least idea of overcharging, like the French. Next day we dined at Cortay, and afterwards crossed the river Sally; and in the afternoon crossed the river Odier to Gibralcon, a large town, where we had good accommodations. When the two Spaniards went to buy corn for the mules, I went along with them. There was a woman of the town who wanted me to pass the night with her. I promised, but I did not perform. But Henry went in place of me. We were very happy here the whole evening. Sir John and I, and the man belonging to the mules, slept in one room; and in the closet, that had no door, slept the master and mistress, and the daughter, a pretty girl, about fifteen. I got up in the night to make water; but, finding no pot, I went to the daughter's bedside, and took her pot. I put it before Sir John's camp-bed; and just before daylight I put it back again; and then I lay down. About six o'clock Henry called us. I made some fine chocolate for Sir John; and after breakfast we set out for St Juan, a long stage of eighteen miles. We stopped at a house on the road, six miles from Gibralcon, to give the mules hay and water; and we ate some hard-boiled eggs, bread and wine, which we always had with us. Soon after, when we were on the road, it began to rain, and continued incessantly the whole day. We had not a place to ſtop at till we came to St Juan. I was obliged to take part of the oilcloth that covered the baggage to hang on Sir John's, on the side next the ſtorm. We had several wine merchants on the road with us.

When we arrived we were put in a house quite empty. The ſtable was part of the house; and the maſter of the house lived next door. His name was Phillips. He kept a shop like a grocer's or chandler's shop in London. He sent us wood for fire, or whatever we wanted. We were there three nights on account of the rain having swelled the rivers so high that we could not pass; there was no bridge nor ferry-boat. Phillips sent whatever we wanted; and was a good, hearty, rich fellow. The third night I was there he dressed me in a Spanish dress, and took me out with him to some of his friends' houses, and to a public-house, where we ſtopped some time.

Next day we were informed the rivers were fallen. We set off for Lucar; and, in the way, we crossed the rivers Tinto and Moncanilla. Lucar is a large city, remarkable for fine churches, which we went to see. It is surrounded by promenades. At this time there was ſtationed at this place a regiment of horse and foot. The officers and ladies were walking together, but the ladies were all veiled. Here Sir John chose to ſtop all night. Next day we went across the plains of Almonte; and at the city of Almonte we dined. In crossing the plains we saw a drove of two thousand hogs, mostly blacks, got from different parts of the country for the great city of Seville. The Spaniards are fonder of hogsflesh than even the English. At night we went to a village called Atalia, near the sea. Here the kitchen and stables were both in one. The mules were at one end and all the strangers at the other. Everyone was his own cook; and I dressed the Queen of Scot's soup. As for the two French gentlemen, we left them in Agamonte. After it was dark at Atalia, the doors were shut, and we were desired not to go out for fear of thieves that lurked in the neighbourhood. Next day we travelled along the seashore to Nepuero, a little village at the bottom of the great river of Guadalquivir. As we had not more than sixteen miles to go that day, we were in no great haste. Sir John and I walked about six miles on the sands, picking up shells of a very fine kind; which were brought to London.

As we were coming to Nepuero, we saw a ship in distress, though it was a very fine day. The ship was no more than a mile from us, and a lee-shore. They did all in their power to get to sea from land, but all in vain. She was loaded with fish from Newfoundland, and was split on a rock near the bottom of the river. Next day we dined at Nepuero, and discharged our men and mules. We had a boat, and crossed the river opposite the custom-house, where the river is two miles over. Our baggage was taken into the custom-house and cleared, and afterwards we had a cart to put it in. We had to walk two miles to the city of St Lucar to the inns, where we had good accommodations and better beds than we had since we left Lisbon. We stopped at St Lucar a week. Sir John stopped with his two friends, Mr Hunter and Mr Carr, wine-merchants. The butler came from Edinburgh; he and I went next morning to see the vessel that was broke to pieces, and we saw the tide drive the fish on shore. The people of St Lucar had a fine chance to get so many thousand fine cod for nothing.

When the gentlemen went out to ride, Mr Hamilton, the butler, and I went out with the two greyhounds a-coursing, and we had very good sport. St Lucar is a very fine city for trade. It stands near the sea, on one of the finest rivers in the world. On the other side are a great many hills, and a fortification about a mile from town. We went into the fort, and there we found English, Irish, Scotch, and Welsh soldiers in the King of Spain's service, and fine easy lives they had, never to stir from St Lucar and the fort. The house where Sir John lodged at St Lucar was one of the largest wine-houses in the town. I went into the wine store-cellars, which resemble a brewer's great store-cellar in London. The morning we left St Lucar, we sent our baggage away in a cart by four in the morning; and we set off by six in the morning. We rode fifteen miles across a fine country, abounding in vineyards and figs. The baggage and we arrived at Port St Mary's by eleven o'clock, at the Three Pigeon's Hôtel, in a very fine town, with a promenade at the end of Port St Mary's for gentlemen and ladies. We dined at the Hôtel, and, as we had but nine miles to Cadiz across the sea, Sir John was very desirous to be there that day, although the wind was very high. I told Sir John that the wind was very high to go in an open boat. He said the boatmen knew beſt. As all the boats were gone that took the regular fare (of about eightpence each person), my maſter engaged one for about eight dollars. When we were making ready to go to the boat, Bernardo, the landlord, an Italian, said; "Mr John, the wind is high, but the men ventured on account of getting so much money". So we went into the large open boat with one maſt and one large sail. The maſter and eight of his men, Sir John, three Spanish gentlemen and Henry and I were on board. We had not proceeded a mile when the wind became very high. In ten minutes it blew a tempeſt : the men, being freshwater sailors, had the sail too high, which laid the boat very much on one side. A sea came and filled the boat half-full of water. When I saw that I made a motion to lower the sail which they did half-way down : if not, the next sea would have swallowed us up. By this time Sir John thought all was over in this life for us, and Henry sat at my feet trembling and speechless. The men had two pails and went to work, to throw the water out of the boat. A wave took away one pail,

and in a few minutes the other pail was carried away
also; then more water came in—everyone in the
boat expected every moment to be lost. The boatmen were crying for their wives and families. I sat
on the windward side of the boat, with my arms on the
rigging, encouraging Sir John, as he had not seen so
much distress as I had seen. The gentlemen were all
on the little deck behind, with the baggage beside
me. Sir John called loudly to the people on board an
English man-of-war to the windward of us, but they
could give us no assistance. I gave myself up for
lost, but I thought within myself, " I shall fare as my
master and no worse". I never saw such a scene.
The men in water up to their middles, crying and
throwing out the water with their hats, and we as
wet as them. I saw no alteration on the Spanish
gentlemen; but they were speaking about Sir John
and me being English, and thought that God had
raised the storm on our account. One of the gentlemen asked if we were English; I answered we were,
and then he asked if we were Catholics of England.
When we were at out wits' end, it pleased God to calm
the wind a great deal. At last we got near the
harbour, and I spoke to Henry, but he could not
answer me a word. Sir John said he had not got the
better of the fright yet. When we got near the Pier of
Cadiz, we had great difficulty to get on shore, as the
waves dashed so much against the Pier. We got
into the little boat from the great one, to take us on
shore, and by the assistance of the rope we got up out

of the boat. There were many hundreds of people glad to see us come safe off the water. Sir John paid the people his compliments by lifting off his hat and making a bow. We went to the White Horse Hôtel all night. At night Sir John sent a letter to his friend, Mr Duff, a great merchant at Cadiz. Mr Duff came home late. In the morning he came to see Sir John and invited him to be at his house while at Cadiz. We went to the house of Mr Duff and Welsh, in company, and next day my master discharged Henry, as he met with an opportunity to go with a gentleman for Lisbon. Next day, as I was dressing Sir John Stuart, he said : " John, I think we escaped wonderfully well with our lives coming from Port St Mary's." " Yes, thank God, I do assure you, Sir John, though I did not show the least marks of fear, I expected every moment to be lost. I thought within myself, I have escaped many dangers, and if I am to die here, I shall fare no worse than my master in death and burying."

Mr Duff was son to the Sheriff of Ayr, in Scotland, and nephew to Mr Hamilton of Bargeny, who brought me up. Mr Hamilton had a brother at that same time in great trade, William Dalrymple, Esq. at Cadiz. In Mr Duff and Welsh's house there were no maidservants, it not being the custom for the single men in Cadiz. In the house were the butler and his mate, as house-man, the headcook and his mate, two Frenchmen and two Italians. I cleaned my master's room and my own, and made our beds, and we were as happy as kings together. There is not so much demand for women-servants in Spain, as there are no fine places—only in the kitchen, and, as in Scotland, the cooks are mostly all men.

Cadiz is as pleasant as any city in Europe : it stands on a peninsula, mostly encompassed by the sea, and fortified all round. The gentlemen and ladies mostly walk on the ramparts for the prospect, and there are seats. There is also a fine promenade under trees, and those that are in carriages go round the promenade, so they can all see one another every afternoon. There are many fine churches in Cadiz. There is a very good custom in Spain. Every evening when the sun sets the bell tolls in all the churches, the men and women stop in a moment, of whatever station, on the promenade or street, while the priests in church say the Lord's Prayer. The men lift off their hats, the ladies put their fans before their face, to pray that God would preserve them through night as he has done through the day, and to thank God for their daily bread. When the oration is done in church the bell tolls again ; then the gentlemen bow to the ladies, and they all walk on again. All carriages and horsemen stopped in the same manner. The priests go about the streets about nine o'clock at night, with lanterns that give a great light, and stop at particular places to pray and praise, to caution people from doing wickedness in the night, and tell them the folly of wickedness and sufferings that follow. The streets are very good in Cadiz, and the houses are high, and make a noble appearance; they are white, built of stone and lime; they are the most convenient in the world for servants. When you enter in the street-door, you are in a square, paved with marble; it is open to the heavens. Round the hall are cellars and warehouses; the stairs are at one corner. When you get up to the first floor, all round are rooms and counting-houses. There is an iron railing round the gallery; the second, third and fourth is in the same manner; so the house is always open. There is a rope fixed to the latch of the street door from the iron railing on each floor, opposite the street-door, so that, whatever place of the house a servant is in, he comes out of the room and looks over the railing, pulls the latch of the street-door with the cord; the person comes in and walks upstairs; then the door falls to again. If it is a message, the servant takes or gives it. When you get on the top of the house, it is flat and pleasant to walk on, or drink tea in the evening. The top of it is finely ornamented with cut stone. Where you walk it is paved with fine flat tiles. In Cadiz there is no water but rain collected from the house-tops; there is indeed water brought from Port St Mary's across the sea, for gentlemen and ladies. Many men support their families by this trade. In the afternoon the men carry a large cask upon their backs, two glasses, and a clean napkin in their hand. They go up to gentlemen and ladies, and sell the company this water. It is pleasing to see so many fine gentlemen and ladies walk on the ramparts and on the promenade, from whence they have so extensive a view both by sea and land. Cadiz is so compact that a man may walk round it in an hour.

All the ladies in the south of Spain, when they walk out, are veiled. As we came to Cadiz before Lent, I fasted the whole time, as they did; but our fast would have been a feast to a Londoner, for we had fine bread and wine, tea and fine butter, and at dinner salt fish, potatoes, parsnips, plenty of sauce, fish stewed in wine, fresh fish boiled, and other fish broiled, eggs fried, and eggs and spinage every day; the gentlemen in the parlour had what they liked besides, for the family was large.

Sir John had not been at Cadiz above three weeks when he was taken ill with an intermittent fever. Mr Macguire, the physician of Cadiz, an Irish gentlemen, attended him. Sir John had no nurse but myself who attended him. I never pulled off my clothes for sixteen nights. I had a fire burning all night, and a lamp to warm everything he wanted. I lay on the couch in the next room. At last he became so weak that he could hardly call me. I said: " Sir if you please, I will put a thing round my wrist in the night, and, when you want me, pull the cord, and I will wake in a moment "; but Sir John rather chose I should lie on the mattress by his bedside; and I did as he desired me. Before three weeks his fever changed and turned to an ague and fever; then he was well sometimes, and then he could walk out, and ride in a carriage. At this time there was a yearly procession, and as it passed by Mr Duff's house, it was very entertaining to my master. It began on Monday and ended on Saturday. It begins with Judas betraying our Lord, and through the week taking Christ before Pilate, and his trial and scourging, and carrying his Cross, and Simon the Cyrenean assisting our Lord to carry the cross, and his being on the Cross between the two thieves, and then left alone, except the Virgin Mary, her sister, and the wife of Cleophas, Mary Magdalen, and John the Beloved. On Saturday Judas throws down the money, and then hangs himself. Those scenes are on stages drawn on wheels. The procession is every day after breakfast performed by several hundreds of the gentlemen in town dressed with their swords and each having a lighted torch in his hand, and accompanied by the priests in grand order.

Sir John getting a little better, Dr Macguire recommended him to the air of Port St Mary's, where he went, and put up at Bernardo's, the Three Pigeons Hôtel, where we were before. My master had a room at the end of the great dining-hall, with two beds; at the other end was General O'Reiley, the Commander-in-Chief of the army in the south part of Spain. The General was an Irishman, and had a grand attendance, though not one British or Irish servant about him. Several of the gentlemen came to see Sir John; and one, Mr Walmsley, an English gentleman who had a fine house and gardens in the country two miles from Port St Mary's, invited Sir John to come and drink milk in the morning, or whatever he liked. My master got a large jackass that belonged to the Hôtel. He put an English saddle on the ass and rode him. We set out at six in the morning. I put my coat over my left shoulder because the weather was hot. I walked, and the ass followed me. This lasted ten days, during which time we returned every day to breakfast. Mr Duff sent his own mule round by land to Port St Mary's; then I rode the ass, and we visited every afternoon different places of the country. No king in the world could enjoy more pleasure than we did, by going from place to place. After General O'Reiley left the Hotel, the Bishop of Seville came to the apartments and dined, on his way to Cadiz.

After three weeks at Port St Mary's, Sir John returned to Cadiz a great deal better—only the ague and fever every three days—and he continued to take the bark. At our return to Cadiz the bull-fights began, the manner of which is as follows: " The theatre is large and round, open overhead; the seats rise from the middle of a grass-plot, like the seats in the two shillings gallery of a play-house; a post is fixed towards one end of the plot, and a baboon chained to it. Before the company came, ten bulls are brought to a stable under the gallery. When the company are come and the Governor and his family seated, a bell rings; the large monkey is on the poſt; three men on horseback, with good boots on, with a large spur in their right hand, ſtand close together abreaſt: one bull is turned out, he ſtamps on the ground, looks at the company, the monkey, and three men on horseback and the three men are ready to receive him. The bull runs full drive at one of the horses; the rider is sure to pierce the bull's shoulder with his spear. He alone muſt attack the bull, and muſt engage him in front. Sometimes the bull throws the man and horse on the ground, at other times he rips up the horse's belly, and you will then see the horse's guts trailing on the ground. When the bull gives the horse the firſt thrust, a person is ready, in a light dress, with a piece of silk of the length of a middling table-cloth; the bull tosses the silk with his horns, and the rider escapes to a place for the purpose. The second time the horsemen get themselves ready again, and the bull, having received the wounds, is more mad than before. Sometimes he runs at the monkey, and then there is a general laugh. When six minutes are over, a bell rings for that scene to finish; then the horsemen ſtand to one side, and another player turns out with two arrows in his hands, each about a yard long, the point sharp like the point of a small fishing-hook. He meets the bull in full gallop, runs the arrow through between his horns, in his shoulders or neck; the bull takes one round in the circus, then another man turns out. The monkey guards his chain, and observes the whole performance. The bull engages the second, third, etc., till he has eight or ten arrows dangling in his back and shoulders; then he is wound up to a great pitch of madness. When the six minutes are over, the bell rings and those men withdraw; then one of the head-performers turns out with an *Andrea Ferara* in his hand, and meets the bull when he is on full gallop. He directs the sword between the horns, down through his shoulders into his heart. The bull falls and expires. In a minute a young man comes with three horses abreast of one another, harnessed and finely decorated with feathers. He fixes the harness round the horns, and drags the carcase full gallop to the slaughterhouse. The meat is sold next day for twopence per pound to the public. Often the swordsmen miss their thrust, and sometimes the bull carries away the sword in his shoulders. At other times, when the swordsman thinks himself sure, he makes a bow to some lady, and says: " In honour of such a lady, I will kill the bull at one thrust." If he succeeds, the company throw down a great deal of money to him; but if not, he is hissed out of the circus.

After being at Cadiz for some time, and Sir John not getting quit of his ague, he laid aside his intended trip to Africa. He resolved to accompany some gentlemen home. He was at a loss at first whether he should go by sea or land, but afterwards preferred the latter. Mr Duff applied to General O'Reiley for an Irish or Scotch soldier to go behind the coach, and be guard and interpreter. Before we got away, we felt an earthquake, on the tenth day of May, in the forenoon. Sir John was laid on his bed; the cook and I were employed in the kitchen. The whole city of Cadiz was somewhat raised and rocked, and sunk again. The cook called on Jesus and Mary; and I cried out: "Jesus Christ! my master will be killed in bed." Every face in Cadiz was as pale as ashes. In ten minutes the people were praying and praising on the streets; however, some tubs were overset.

Two days after, we went to Port St Mary's, and a great many gentlemen in company, who stopped all night with my master at Bernardo's. In a few days after, my master hired a coach and six mules that was going to Madrid. He found there were orders for everyone to join their regiment, as the French were expected to join the Americans; so that General O'Reiley would not let Sir John have a soldier. So we went without an interpreter or guard. We left the pleasant place Port St Mary's with our coach and six mules, worth sixty or seventy guineas each.

About the middle of May we set out for Madrid, three hundred and fifty miles distant. We went very little faster than a waggon in England. We only went one short stage the first night, to Xeres, the principal town for sherry-wine in Spain. Great respect is paid to gold lace; and I was mistaken, at the inns, for Sir John. I begged of my master to wear some of his gold-laced clothes, which he did all through Spain. The inns were tolerable; and the waiter laid the cloth for Sir John and me. I supped with Sir John for the first time; and slept in the same room till we came to St Jean de Luz, in France. Next morning early we set out for Arcos. We commonly set out by four, to travel in the cool of the morning. On the road, when we were let into an empty room, where we were taken no notice of, I was cook; the maid would get me water, and make a fire. I had a case of fine wine for my master, and sherry for myself; I had spices, salt, and rice, and a little copper-pot with a shelf at top for the meat. I dressed the dinner for next day. I had soup in the bottom of the pot and the fowl at top; the cover came half-way down the outside, so that no dust could get in. At dinner-time I had only to warm the dinner. I hung the pot under the perch of the coach by a rope. I could buy partridges, fowls, chickens, eggs, and some fish, which I stewed in wine. We commonly had our luncheon on the road; the coachman and his nephew on the box would eat theirs, and we in the coach ours; we commonly had cold broiled chicken or some partridge. As I dressed plenty, Sir John desired me to give the master of the coach part, out of the window; so we were all at luncheon together, and going slow. I made chocolate overnight to drink at four in the morning. Sir John never had a return of the ague on the road, which made the journey very pleasing, and no man upon earth more happy than me, travelling through a fine country where the harvest was all in by the twentieth of May. At night we slept in the town of Bornos. Nothing remarkable but merriment. Our coachman was a fine handsome man, and he and his nephew were very fond of dancing. A person came with the guitar ; and he danced with the mistress of the house and another girl. It cost me many a shilling to pay for music, travelling along. Very few days but he and his nephew dined at every stage we stopped at.

Next morning we dined at Espera, after passing the mountains of Alhoquina. We left Espera and travelled along a fine country, well cultivated, finely wooded, and watered, and at night we came to a fine town called Utera, and then to Marchina. From thence we came at night to a fine city called Exija, leaving the great city of Seville on our left hand. Here we crossed a branch of the river Guadlaquivir, and went to Palma to dinner ; and we crossed another branch of the river, and stopped at the town of Pasados. We were here early in the evening. The people of the inns were relations of Prosilla, the coachman. Sir John was very glad to see Prosilla dance. He always put a rattle on each hand, which kept time to the music. As Sir John was very glad to see him, he himself danced a fandango. I went to the church every place we came at, and I passed for a Roman Catholic. They asked me if my master was a Roman Catholic : I said he was. " It is Friday, and you are dressing a fowl for him ? " I told them, when my master was at St Lucar he went to see the High Priest, and desired to be permitted to eat meat as he was travelling through Spain for his health. The High Priest gave my master an indulgence to eat any sorts of birds while in Spain, for which my master gave the poor of St Lucar one hundred dollars, and my master has it in his pocket-book. That night I made an East India pilaw for my master. I had a fine fowl stewed with rice and butter, well-seasoned. I had hard-boiled eggs, and boiled onions to garnish the dish. When it was making ready, the landlady was taken ill. I told Sir John. He desired me to take her a glass of brandy. She drank it. When I served in the supper, Sir John sent her a large plate full of pilaw, and desired her to eat as she was a fellow-sufferer with himself, and indeed she eat hearty. I had fish for my supper. Prosilla and the others in company laughed hearty to themselves that the land-lady was sick and ate and drank heartily. If a person be sick, he is allowed to eat meat at that time, although it is in Lent, or on Friday. We left Pasados in the morning, and dined at the great city of Cordova, on the river Guadalquivir. Before my master had dinner we went to see a fine church that had seven hundred pillars of marble in the middle. After dinner we went to Samossa, after crossing the mountains of Constantina covered with flowers of different colours. When I saw a flower or plant that was strange to me,

I took the seed and dried it by the sun, and brought it with me to send to Scotland. Next morning we left Samossa, and dined at St Bennet's in the province of New Caſtile. In the afternoon we went over the mountains of Conoviſta, and ſtopped at the town of Gorgortial, a fine town in a beautiful country. We ſtopped at a very good inn, and the maid was good-tempered. I dressed the supper, and the maid and I drank a bottle of wine together. When she brought in the supper, I was setting up my maſter's tent bed. Sir John began to eat his supper. The maid said: "Why do you begin before your comrade?" My maſter said: "John, I see I can by no means begin till you come, without disobliging the maid." I put on my coat in a minute and sat down to supper. As I made the chocolate at night, she showed me where she slept, that I might call her in the morning. When I came to her bedside, before I called her, I took up her pockets and put in one dollar. Methinks a good-natured person should be respeᴄted and rewarded. I said: "My dear, I beg your pardon, but I have called you an hour too soon." She said: "There is no harm done. Do you lay down till I make the fire and warm the chocolate, and when it is ready, I will let you know." We went to dinner to Uenta del Aleada, and at night we slept at a large town called Villa Major, at a good inn. That night there was a great deal of rain, thunder, and lightning; but within, very agreeable, and plenty of music and danc- ing; and the landlady was a great while conversing

with my maſter. After she was gone, I said : " Sir,
the gentlemen of Cadiz laughed at me because I said
we had no kind of need of an interpreter. You see,
Sir John, I was right ; there would have been the
man's expense, and he would have made them charge
you double for everything on the road." Sir John
said : " In a few months I could speak Spanish as well
as French ; it is half Latin, and I speak Latin as well
as French." When we were going to bed, it
thundered very much. Sir John said : " I believe
there is not any one thing bad but I have met with since
I left home." " Sir ", said I, " If some of the old
Scotchwomen were here, they would say : ' Certainly
Sir John has forsaken some young lady that he has
such bad luck.' " I said this because I was informed
that he had forsaken one of the fineſt young ladies
in Scotland, an heiress, and took up with another
heiress as good as the other, whom he married afterwards. He made me no answer, for he knew what I
said was right.

Next day we passed a fine country, and crossed
a branch of the river Guadiana, and stopped at the
town of Luciana. After dinner we went over the
mountains of Luciana, and ſtopped at the town of
Piedrabuena, a fine country, near a large ridge of
mountains. There is no danger of thieves in Spain.
As you ſtop in towns or villages, you may leave five
hundred pounds worth in your coach all night,
without any danger ; but the banditti on the mountain

or in large woods are dangerous. Next day we dined
at Mora. After passing the mountains of Mora and
Cole, on a Saturday night, we arrived at the large
and fine city of Toledo. We were at a good inn and
we had good accommodations. Here we crossed
the river Tagus, that runs paſt Lisbon. We were in
no great hurry to go off in the morning, as we had
only one ſtage to dinner, and to be there all night—
the place where the King of Spain had his court.
When Sir John was dressed and gone down to breakfaſt, I was shaving and dressing myself, when the maid
came to make the bed ; and conversing together, she
asked me to shave her. I said : " My dear, suppose it
should spoil your pretty face." " Sir, you shave, and
your face is not spoiled." " Very well, my dear, if
you will give me a kiss, I will shave you." So she
gave me a kiss, and I shaved her ; and I told her she
was the firſt maid I had ever shaved. She was about
sixteen, and I was very sorry to leave her behind.
After breakfaſt we set out, and arrived at Aranjuez,
the moſt beautiful village I ever saw. Before we
came to Aranjuez, we were going over the moſt barren
hill in Spain, and presently we saw before us the moſt
pleasant valley, about ten miles long. At the bottom
of the hill is the town, the moſt complete building, of
white hewn ſtone, every ſtreet answering another
like the walls of a garden, planned before a house was
built. The King's palace is at the side of the town,
a beautiful building, on the banks of the river Tagus,
at the end of a fine, white, ſtone bridge, across the

river, in the King's delightful pleasure-garden, open for the public to walk in. We ſtopped at the King's Arms. When our things were taken upſtairs, I, having nothing to do, walked out. I saw the people going to the King's chapel, where the Queen and one of the Princesses were in the royal seat. As I was very well dressed, and had a silk bag on my hair and a fine hanger by my side, I entered the chapel. When the service was over, I came home. When Sir John was at dinner, I told him I had been at the chapel. He was attended by two Spanish waiters. He was well served, they knowing him to be an Englishman, the English bearing the charaĉter of being so rich and free. My maſter said : " John, I have been counting how many dishes they will bring to me. In all, I have had fourteen hot things." When my maſter was speaking to me, the two waiters looked at my maſter and me, I said : " Sir, I will go and see what I ſhall have below." I went and dined, and told Sir John I had eleven hot things for my dinner.

My maſter sent a letter to Lord Grantham, the English Ambassador, to let him know such a person was at the King's Arms. I went and saw the King's gardens, and returned to tell Sir John the beauty of them. He went to see them, and returned, expeĉting the Earl of Grantham's answer ; but I went along the road, and walked outside of the Queen's gardens, between the river and the great road leading to Madrid. It is near half a mile long, and half a quarter of a mile broad, open to view from the road by a low wall and fine iron railing; but the public are not allowed to enter. It produces all sorts of plants and fine flowers to put into the Queen's apartments and in different places of the palace, and there are many fine trees growing between the river and garden. The great road by the garden has fine trees on each side, like those in St James's Park, London, where the ladies walk in the afternoon. This road is watered twice on each day, at the King's expense. The royal family come here an-airing sometimes, and the nobles and gentry come here in the cool of the afternoon. I have seen five hundred carriages at once. At accustomed places they drive along one side of the road and down the other. There are gentlemen and ladies on the footway, between the carriages and the Queen's gardens; so they are all together, and not the least dust to be seen, the roads being so well watered. One would not wish to see a finer sight than the company. I went to the other side of the garden, and I saw one of the gardeners coming from the building for the gardeners, and enter a backdoor of the garden. I went and found the door on the latch. I entered. and walked along the gravel walk. When I came near the gardeners it being Sunday, they were looking at some flowers, not at work. They looked at me, and, seeing me to be a foreigner and knowing how I came in, they took no farther notice. I walked round, and saw some fine walks of trees and flowers. I put some flowers in my pocket, and walked out and came home to Sir John, and gave him the flowers from the Queen's garden. He asked me how I got in there. I told him I had gone into many places that was not allowed for the public, because I was a stranger. He answered: "You had better take care and not get into trouble by so doing." Late at night Sir John had a letter from Lord Grantham, and waited on him next day; dined with his lordship, and went to court. As I never saw a place I liked so well; at the same time I went to see the King's stables, the horseguards, and the King's dairy, the finest in Europe. The King of Spain supplies all the ambassadors with butter, milk and cream, from his dairy, while he is in the country. If there be a place in the world at this time like the garden of Eden, it is Aranjuez. When Sir John came home, he told me what he had seen at the court, and how much the English ambassador was respected by all the other ambassadors. Sir John said; "I would like to stay here longer, but I have to pay Prosilla the coachman one pound per day while I stay here". After four days at Aranjuez, we set out for Madrid. We went five miles down the east side of the river; then crossed one of the finest bridges I ever saw out of the county of Middlesex. When we left the valley, we went up a high hill to the west, and left the delightful valley of Aranjuez. We went on for Madrid, twenty-one miles; but we stopped at Leganes to bait, the custom of Spain. When we were on our way to Madrid, if we met a carriage going to Aranjuez, we were obliged to give way. We crossed another branch of the river Tagus, and put up at the St Sebastian, an elegant hôtel, the master of which was an Italian. Next day my master hired a coach for himself and two English gentlemen. The Earl of Grantham's chaplain accompanied them to see the King's palace, the armoury, and his cabinet of curiosities. I went on behind the coach, and saw everything that was worth seeing in Madrid. When we were looking out of the palace windows in Madrid, we saw the Escurial, a palace twenty-one miles north from Madrid. At the same time we saw the distant mountains covered with snow, though it was then the beginning of June, After viewing everything worth seeing, the gentlemen stopped at Lord Grantham's town-house. Sir John desired me to go home, as I had the key of the room where they were to dine, and get the table ready for dinner. I went, but lost my way. I was in the greatest perplexity of mind, as I had the key of all the things and of the room, and I had forgot the name of the hôtel. I walked up one street and down another ; at last I remembered the name of the hôtel. I went up to a Spaniard and asked him for the St Sebastian. He answered : " I do not understand you, because I do not know the name of the street." I asked for the hôtel, but could not give the street. At last I went up to a French gentleman, who put me right presently, and I got home before Sir John and his company. Next day we saw the grand procession, such as we saw at Cadiz, but much grander. The street where the procession went through was covered with canvas, fixed to the three pair of stairs windows, in case of rain; but it happened to be fine weather. Madrid is a fine city, in a beautiful country. Madrid is lighted up with glass lamps like London. In Madrid the women wear white veils. After being four nights in Madrid, we set out for the Escurial. On our way we only ſtopped a few minutes at a watering-house, and arrived at the Escurial by noon; there we had time to see the palace and village. About two miles before you come to the Escurial, you ascend, as the palace ſtands on a fine height, the moſt beautiful rural place in the world. The palace is one of the longeſt in Europe, in figure like a gridiron; the handle in a fine garden, and the part of the palace like the gridiron is a fine square where carriages drive, very much resembling Holyrood House, the royal palace in Scotland. We went to see the king's chapel, and the fine painting; one drew my maſter's attention, and that was the conversion of Paul. The friars were at prayers when we were in the chapel, and were sur-prised to hear me name all the paintings exaĉtly. Next morning we travelled through a country like a garden, till we began to ascend the high mountains. We were to cross to get out of the province of New Caſtile into Old Caſtile. I got out of the coach to make it easier for the mules. I was sometimes half a mile before the mules, because I went ſtraight forward. I had milk from the shepherds out of a large horn; and I met Sir John at a corner of the road. Near the top of the mountains we entered into a cloud, it was so thick and dark. Sir John called me to come into the coach to give him the bark. When we left the mountains behind, we got into a fine country, and arrived at a large town called Idelfonso in Old Caſtile. Here we ſtopped all night on account of the beauty of the place. It is situated in a fine valley between the high mountains of Brides. Next morning we went to Segovia, a fine town, with fine houses. At night we went to St Maria de la Nieve, in a fine, well-cultivated country, with many fine woods, and passed by some convents. Next day we dined at Olmedo, and arrived at night at Valdeſtillas. I took more delight in seeing the north part of Spain than the south, because it afforded so many hills, valleys, rivers and woods. Next morning we set out for Valladolid, a great city, but poor buildings, with an old palace of the Kings of Spain, with a cathedral and fine paintings. We ſtopped to dinner, then set out for Duenas. This part of Spain is barren, and the people poor, not having trade. Next morning we went to Torquenado, and at night to Villadrigo. Next day to dinner at Quintanillaja, and at night to the large city of Burgos, the capital of Old Caſtile. This city is very rich and grand. It ſtands on the banks of the river Alençon, and here is a fine cathedral, with excellent paintings. Sir John ſtopped here two days, because he met some English gentlemen. We were there on the market-day, which gave us an opportunity of seeing more of the humour of the place. The country round is fine and well-culti-vated. We left Burgos, and travelled over the very high mountains of Bribiesca, through bad roads. We had dinner at Bodilles, and at night arrived at Bribiesca. Afterwards we had a beautiful country to go through, but bad roads to pass. As we were going along, I observed a house like Fullarton's Folly in Scotland. Sir John looked round, and said: "I never saw a finer sight; such a fine country, and fine river." "Sir," said I, "there is a finer sight in Scotland." He said: "Where, for God's sake?" "Sir, from the castle of Stirling. If young noblemen and gentlemen would take notice of Great Britain and Ireland before they went on their travels, it would make a good foundation for their remarks." Next day we dined at Pancorva, and pursued our journey through the mountainous country of Mirando, and through a great many woods. We had a guard with us for one stage. At this time we were very happy with our coachman and postilion, and we had plenty of music and dancing. Although the harvest was in when we left Cadiz, they were only weeding their fields of green corn in the north of Spain. We dined at Vittoria; whence we set out for Mondrogone. On this stage we entered the great mountain of the Pyrenees, which runs from the Bay of Biscay to the Mediterranean Sea, and, upon an average, is fifty miles broad, and covered constantly with snow. On the stage between Mirando and Victoria we crossed the river Ebro, and entered the province Biscay. When we entered first between two rocks, there was only room for the coach to pass. We were three days in passing the Pyrenees, the road serpentined so much, to get round the mountains. We ſtopped at Villafranca. Next day we dined at Tolosa. It was very pleasant travelling through the valleys to see the snow on the mountains, while the valley was as warm as France or Spain. We travelled by a river the whole day; and there were plenty of trees on the side of the mountains. At night we ſtopped at Ogarzin, the pleasanteſt place I ever saw. At this town the valley was very narrow, and mountains very high, the sides covered with cheſtnut-trees. In passing the Pyrenees we had the beſt white wine I ever drank. In the morning we left Ogarzin, and went to the river Bidassoa, which divides Spain and France. The river is deep, but not very broad. We crossed over all at once in a ferryboat, and we had our things taken to the cuſtom-house to be searched. On the one side they spoke French, on the other side Spanish. Here we entered Gascony, and dined at St Jean de Luz.

Sir John and I began to separate dining or sleeping in one room together; and here I left my kitchen-furniture behind, not having any more occasion for them at night. We ſtopped at Bayonet, a large trading city on the great river Adour. I was surprised to see the people in Gascony; I thought I was in Scotland, for the people dress in the same manner, with short coats and blue bonnets, and there is not the leaſt difference in their behaviour. As Prosilla, the coach-maſter had fulfilled his engagements for his coach

and mules, he was paid off. I was sorry to part with
him and his nephew, and he was sorry to part with
Sir John and me. Next day Sir John bought a French
post-chaise, and they both saw us set off post for
Bourdeaux. We dined at a large town called Deux
on the river Adour, and at night arrived at Lesperon.
This country had a great many woods and bad roads.
Next day to St Julian, next day to Escourse, and slept
at Castress; next day to Bourdeaux, and put up at the
Hôtel de Richelieu, near the grand promenade and the
new playhouse. As there were a great many British
and Irish gentlemen here, Sir John said he would stop.
He ordered a chariot with a coachman and footman,
and jaunted through the city of Bourdeaux, one of the
finest places in France for beauty and for trade. It
is a great resort for company; it is above two miles
long, on the river Garonne, on which you will see
ships of all countries. Most of the country is vineyards, as it is the country where claret is made. After
we had been there one week, the mistress of the hotel,
her brother, a master-shoemaker, and an English
housekeeper, a French valet, and I made a party on a
Sunday to go to the mistress's brother, three miles down
the river, on the other side, at Madam Reives's
brother's house. As soon as we were in the boat
Madam Reives took a pack of cards out of her pocket
to play. She desired me for her partner. I made
many excuses against it, but all would not do, as she
had seen me play before. I apologized, and in all my
life I have never done so before, nor never had done

any thing on a Sunday that gave me so much uneasiness before; for I always regarded the Sunday; but they were all Roman Catholics: dancing or gambling on Sunday, they think no harm. When we came to Madam Reives's brother's, we walked in the vine-yards, on the banks of the river. We ate grapes, drank wine, had fish of the river stewed in wine, and in the evening we returned by water at sunset. At this time, the Emperor of Germany was making the tour of France, accompanied by the Count of Provence, the King of France's brother, and many other noblemen. The day they arrived at Bourdeaux two of the noblemen came to our hôtel. Three days after I was at the gate of the hôtel at nine in the morning, when I saw the Emperor and all his attendants going to mass. I went directly without putting on my hat, and got into church. Thousands of people flocked in the ſtreets to see the Emperor. He did not ſtop long at mass. As he was coming out of church, he spoke to the Count de Provence, as he thought he would be obſtructed getting out, the people thronged so much about the church. The Emperor went out with one of his lords, and, as the people knew neither of them, both of them went into the nobleman's chariot, and drove off. Soon after, the Earl of Provence and the other lords came out and drove away. The Emperor's carriage drove away empty. The people asked the coachman who was the Emperor. He said that he went away in the firſt carriage, so they were disappointed. I got out of the crowd, came home, and called my

mafter at ten o'clock; and I told him I had been at
mass with the Emperor and the Count de Provence,
and what I had seen. He said: "I wish I had been
there to see the Emperor and the Earl of Provence."
After we were two weeks at Bourdeaux, Sir John made
a party to go to Bagneres, at the bottom of the
Pyrenees. The party was my mafter, Edward Coke,
Esq., Captain Fagan, in the French service, belonging
to a regiment of horse and of the Order of St Louis,
Captain Woolley, an Irish gentleman, and Mr Hooper,
an American gentleman. In the middle of July we
left Bourdeaux, and dined at Coftress, and went at
night to Langon, a fine town, in a fine country.
Next to Marmonde, then to Tormaine, Aqillion, and
Agen, poft-towns, and at night to Leirace. Next
morning we went to Leytaure, changed horses;
then to Auch, and then at night to Tarble. This town
is a fine large market-town, in a fine country, surrounded with vineyards, on a branch of the river
Adour. Next day we arrived at Bagneres. The
gentlemen went to housekeeping; they had the
Mayor's house, they had a man cook, kitchen maid, and,
as the Mayor lived in the house, his maid cleaned the
rooms and took care of her mafter's things. As Mr
Coke's servant and I were British, we did the work one
week, and the French servants another, Bagneres is
like the German Spa, for company for all places.
They drink the water, ride out, some on horseback,
others in carriages, meet to play cards, have balls,
and there are fine walks round the town. It is a sweet

place, for the waters of the river run through every house in town; so all filth is carried away. This place lies one hundred miles eaſt of Baysmet, at the bottom of the Pyrenees. The town is very hot, though when looking out of your windows you can see the snow on the top of the mountains. Sometimes the company dined in the wood or in a grove. When they came to the place, some walked about, others played cards till dinner-time, everyone speaking the French language.

On the first of Auguſt, when Sir John was of age, he gave a dinner to the gentlemen and ladies at Bagneres, near fifty people up the valley, between the Pyrenees, at a village called Compa. On both sides, some of the mountains, like sugar loaves, were two or three miles high, covered with snow, and below as hot as you can bear it. The dinner was fine, and plenty of fine wines and card-playing; but, unluckily for Sir John, after dinner, when he went into the necessary house, he left his repeating-watch behind him, a new gold one of the firſt sort. The watch and chain, etc., was valued at one hundred guineas. Inquiry was made but all to no purpose. A reward was offered to any person that would deliver it; but all in vain. Our gentlemen ſtopped here till the end of Auguſt, and then went to Barege, about fifteen miles further up amongſt the Pyrenees. Bagneres is only on the side of the mountain. Barege is as much frequented as Bagneres is, like Bath and Briſtol. The gentlemen left Barege after dinner, and were all night at Purre-selt, near leaving the mountains. Next day we dined at Louredes, a beautiful town amongst vineyards. We cut the grapes off with our hangers as we were riding along; and late at night we came to Tarbe, a fine large market town. Next day was a great fair. The gentle-men stopped here one day, as Mr Hooper and Captain Woolley were to part with my master and Mr Cooke and Captain Fagan. Next day after we went for Bourdeaux, and in two days arrived there. Sir John stopped one week at Bourdeaux, and set out for Paris. We crossed the great river Garonne at Bourdeaux in a boat, and at the next stage, Cubsac, we crossed another branch of the river in a ferry-boat, and went post to Molieu; then Barbescieux, through a fine wine country; then to Moli all night. In the morning we crossed the river Charente in a ferryboat; as the road was good, and very good horses, we went on very quick. We went to Russee, to Viome, and to Potiers; and at night we crossed a branch of the river Loire, and slept all night at the fine large town of Chatellrault, whence the Duke of Hamilton has his French dukedom. At this time there was a great many company in town and at our hôtel where we put up, and of course I was at supper with a great many servants. The custom of the hôtel was, the servants that came last sat lowest at table. When supper was over, I took off my hat and put it before my face, and said grace; then crossed myself and put my hat on again; took up the bread and kissed it, and then put it on the table. All the servants looked at me, and they took off their hats out of complaisance to me, and put them on again, for the French servants are very respectful to anything religious. They asked me if my master was a Bishop. I said, "No, he was a gentleman on his travels". They said : " From what country, pray Sir ? " " From Scotland, gentlemen. My master is Sir John Stuart. His family is sprung from the kings of Scotland " ; by this they thought Sir John and I must be very religious, for they spake of King Charles the First losing his life for religion.

We set off next morning for St Maure. On this stage we crossed another branch of the river Loire. From St Maure we crossed three branches of the Loire, next to Veue, then we went and dined at the city of Blair. After dinner, to Bengeney, through pleasant country ; and at night to Orleans city, a fine large and beautiful place on the river Loire. Next morning early we left the city of Orleans and the river Loire behind us. Nothing remarkable happened, but we were passing through a fine country, with good entertainment. Our next post was Arteny ; then to Etampes ; then to dinner at Arpajon ; and at night to Paris, and put up at the Hôtel de Saxe Rue Faubourg St Germaine. Next day Sir John had a large coachman and footman to visit his friends. He found a great many young gentlemen of his acquaintance, which induced him to stay longer than he intended. We arrived in Paris about the end of September, and we

ſtopped eight weeks at the Hôtel de Saxe. We went
to all public places, and he kept the firſt company in
Paris; and we servants lived like princes. We left
Paris on St Andrew's Day, a day that is kept more
holy in France than Sunday. We went post by
Chantillie, Amiens, Abbeville, and in two days arrived
at Boulogne, at my maſter's uncle's house. Mr Seton
was one of the firſt men in the wine-trade in the uni-
verse. Sir John ſtopped here three weeks. Boulogne
is a pleasant town on the seaside, within two ſtages of
Calais and in sight of England, on the great poſt
road from Calais to Paris. We went by sea from
Boulogne to Dover. Sir John left his French poſt-
chaise at Boulogne, and we arrived in London the
firſt day of January, 1778, at Mrs Elliot's house in
Brewer Street, Golden Square. Sir John was in
perfeçt health; he ſtopped in London one week; and,
as he was desirous of seeing his relations in Scotland
and having no further occasion for me, he paid me off.
He desired me to send his baggage by sea, and he went
with a gentleman in a poſt-chaise to Allan Bank, in
Berwickshire, in Scotland; so we parted, and I was
out of place. I took things very easy, as it was a
good time of the year to get one. I went after none
but a place with a single man, as I wanted for nothing.
I had my own lodging, with my own furniture; and
whether I was at home or abroad, I paid my good old
landlady, a widow-woman; and she made of it what
she could in my absence: therefore she took care of
my goods. I dressed in the same manner I went

abroad. Having good clothes, with rich vests, I wore
my hanger, a silk bag at my hair, and laced ruffles ; but,
when I went after a place, I dressed in the common way.
If it rained, I wore my fine silk umbrella : then the
people would call after me : " What, Frenchman,
why do you not get a coach ? " In particular, the
hackney coachmen and hackney chairmen would call
after me ; but I, knowing the men well, went straight
on, and took no notice. At this time there was no
umbrellas worn in London, except in noblemen's
and gentlemen's houses ; where there was a large one
hung in the hall, to hold over a lady or gentleman
if it rained, between the door and their carriage. I
was going to dine in Norfolk Street, one Sunday. It
rained ; my sister had hold of my arm ; and I had the
umbrella over our heads. In Tavistock Street we
met so many young men, calling after us : " Frenchman ! take care of your umbrella." " Frenchman,
why do you not get a coach, Monsieur ? " My sister
was so much ashamed that she quitted my arm and ran
on before, but I still took no notice but answered in
French or Spanish that I did not understand what they
said. I went on so for three months, till they took
no further notice of me, only " How do you do
Frenchman ? " After this the foreigners, seeing me
with my umbrella, one after another used theirs—then
the English. Now it is become a great trade in London,
and a very useful branch of business. When I went
to a public-house where servants meet in the evenings
I was called by the name of " Beau Macdonald " or

the "Scotch Frenchman". I went sometimes to the
Seven Stars, Eagle Street, Piccadilly, which is frequented only by foreigners. They asked me from what
country. I said from Cadiz in Spain. You may be
twenty years in London and not meet with a Spanish
servant. In the month of March there was a house-
warming at Knightsbridge. A gentleman's servant
took a public-house, and he asked his friends to come.
There was a supper and ball. Thirty men and twenty-
two women came. I was one of the company, which
was very genteel, from noblemen and gentlemen's
houses of different countries. The Mafter of the
ceremonies was a Scotchman, who delighted more in
that ftation than in the Prayer Book. The evening
was spent very agreeably by the company at country-
dances, cards and drinking. Supper was at eleven
o'clock. After supper the company came into the
drawing-room and began again. As I had not danced
in the evening, I asked the ladies if they would do me
the honour to dance a minuet with me, as I had no
partner. They all answered they could not dance a
minuet, till at laft I came to the wife of a serjeant of the
King's Body Guards, a genteel woman. She under-
ftood dancing well; she untucked the skirts of her
gown. I called for 'Miss Carmichael's minuet'.
I let the tune be played over once, that the gentle-
woman might underftand the minuet. While we
ftood at the end of the room for the minuet to begin,
the company got up from their card-tables and their
drinking. As there had been no minuet before in

the evening, they gave great attention. When we had danced the minuet, I asked the favour of the lady to dance a jig; she answered she would. She buttoned up the skirts of her gown, and I called for 'Lady Kitty Carstair's Reel'. We both danced together in the form of the minuet, though quick. When we were done, the company called "Encore, encore" I asked the lady if it was agreeable to dance again. She answered: "Yes." "Then, madam, choose your tune." She said: "The same again." I thought within myself, what agreeable creatures those women are; they are not changeable; if they like a tune a man dances with them, they do not want to change from it. We went through our dance as before, and I treated her and the ladies with a bottle of sweet mountain. In this month of March I called at Lowe's Hotel, Covent Garden. As I went in, the waiter told me: " Macdonald, I was just going to send a porter for you. I have an excellent place for you. A gentleman here, going abroad; his name is James O'Neil, Esq., a very fine young man, in his twenty-first year. His father is a man of great fortune in Ireland. He served his time to the wine-trade in Dublin; now he is going to the wine-countries to make connections and to know the customs abroad. I heard him tell a gentleman, he would not have a foreign servant, because sometimes, when they get what they can in England, they rob their masters and leave them. Well, it is an old saying: An Irish gentleman will not be imposed upon." The waiter

told Mr O'Neil: " The servant he mentioned to us
in the hall." " Call him in." I went in. He asked
me what countryman. I said a North Briton. After
asking me some questions he hired me. After this
Mr O'Neil stopped at London two weeks to see the
places in London, and dining at one place in the
country, then at another—Richmond, Hampton
Court, Windsor, Shooter's Hill, etc. Then we set
out post for Bath, put up at the Three Tuns, and
stopped there two weeks ; then my master told me to
take two changes of linen with me, and order a post-
chaise below : I want to go to see Bristol. We put up
at Mrs Perry's, Queen's Square ; stopped here one
day, and returned to Bath. Afterwards we set out
post for Wells, Bridgewater, Taunton, Tiverton,
then to Exeter. Next day we set out for Plymouth,
and stopped a few days, and then went round for
Falmouth. We waited for a fair wind only two days.
There was a great many passengers. English gentlemen and ladies going to Lisbon for pleasure as well
as their health ; from England, Scotland, Ireland, and
Wales. We sailed in the *Expedition*, Captain
Robertson, with a fair wind. We got to Lisbon in
fourteen days. We saw several ships, but never
hailed one, they being not near enough. Everything
was agreeable on the passage, and the company very
happy. There was a lady from Cornwall, with a
beautiful daughter, about sixteen, and her son in a
decline, about nineteen years old. The day we first
saw the rock of Lisbon, the young gentleman died ;

MEMOIRS OF AN

his corpse was carried on shore, and buried in the
English burying-place. He was heir to a large eſtate
in Cornwall. When we arrived at Lisbon, the company went to the English Hôtel. My maſter had the
same equipage, man and horse, that Sir John Stuart
had. We were in Lisbon six weeks; then the company made a party and went to Syntra, to the north-
ward of the Tagus, near the seaside, a pleasant place.
Here the company enjoyed themselves by going out an-
airing in view of the sea and the rock of Lisbon. In a
week we returned to Lisbon, and in two days bought
our travelling-bed and other utensils as before when
with Sir John Stuart. I called my maſter to see the
different things, which seemed ſtrange to him. He
asked me where my bed was. "Sir, I have none; I
take my chance." He hired a chaise and two mules
to carry the baggage—they were already at Aldea
Gallega. We crossed the Tagus, and ſtopped there
all night at the house where I was at with Sir John.
In the morning we set out for Pegoens, through a fine
country; then to Ventas Nuecvas. We ſtopped all
night. I went a-cocking. Mr O'Neil was surprised
to see the difference between Portugal and England or
Ireland. I ate with my maſter, and slept in the same
room, through Portugal and Spain, as I did with Sir
John Stuart. We had the driver and the baggage-man
with the two mules, but no interpreter. Next day to
Ventas Silveras, and dined at Montemor Novi; and
at night to Arrazolas, a fine town in a beautiful country
for wines, oranges and lemons. In the town is a royal

palace. Next morning to Evoramonte, a small town ;
and at night to Elvas, which is a ſtrong fortified town
on the confines of Portugal. Next morning we set out
for Badajoz. On this ſtage we left Portugal, and
entered Spain. Badajoz is the capital of the province
of Eſtremadura, a very large, ſtrong, fortified city
where there are a great many troops. At leaving the
city of Badajoz, we crossed the river Guadiana.
Next we passed through Talavera ; next we passed
through Lobon, and at night to Merida, a fine
city, with fine churches and grand buildings with
very grand and genteel company. As my maſter,
was of the Church of Rome, we were very agreeable
to the people, and they to us, as we travelled along.
Next day we passed through Buixellanes and San
Pedro, where we dined. Here we entered the
province of New Caſtile, a fine town ; and at night
to Mujadas. Next day to Puerto de Santa Cruz, and
at night to Trasillo. Here was one of the fineſt
churches in Spain—a fine town, where we had good
accommodation. Next day we went to Serezejo, a fine
town, with fine buildings. On this road, the mountains
were so high, that we were obliged to get two
oxen to help the horses over the mountains. We
walked on foot. Next we came to Casas del Puerto ;
then to Venta Nueva, a town with very fine buildings.
We left this and crossed the Tagus river, over which
is a very fine bridge of twelve arches. We ſtopped all
night at Almarez, where we had very good and civil
accommodation. As my maſter spoke the Spanish

and French as well as Latin, and that before he left Lisbon he had a very rich Spanish dress made trimmed with gold, everyone took him for a Spaniard. If ever there was an angel of a man, he was one. He allowed the men their provision from his own good nature. He never did anything without speaking to me for my advice ; and wherever there was music, at any of the ſtages, he always paid them for playing, which made us always merry. I thought my life was heaven upon earth. Next morning we passed Espadanal ; then Naval Moral Valparido ; and dined at Calcada de Oropea ; then through Toralca, and at night to Ventta de Peral Benegas, fine towns in a fine country, and the most harmless people in the world. Next day we dined at the city of Talavera de Regna, a place of great trade. My maſter and I went to see all the churches, and a number of fine buildings ; and we also went to see a great many manufaċtories, for which the place is famous. After dinner we passed through Venta Del Alverche ; and at night to Bravo. Although the city of Toledo was out of our way, I had a great desire to go through it. I told my maſter : " If you please, sir, to go by Toledo ; it is one of the fineſt cities in Spain, and, going from thence to Madrid, you will see Aranjuez, where the King of Spain keeps his Court part of the year—one of the fineſt places in Europe, Sir." He said : " I should be glad to see Aranjuez " ; so he desired the poſtilion next morning to drive to Montalbar, where we dined ; and at night to Toledo. This whole day we were going by the side of the river Tagus that washes Madrid, Toledo, Aranjuez, and Lisbon—the pleasanteſt journey ever a man travelled. As we were in Toledo at four in the afternoon, Mr O'Neil went to see the churches, and I with him. When I came back I inquired for Malilia, the girl that was there laſt year. They told me she was at her father's and went away with child to an Englishman that was travelling the road with his maſter; and that, as the servant's name was John, they called the child John England. I asked what her father was; they said he was a cooper and cousin to our maſter. I desired to be taken to her father's house. They said: "Sir, I suppose you are the father of the boy." The landlord came out directly, and all the people looked at me, and said: "This is the child's father, God help her, dear girl." I was taken to her father's house, and when I entered the child was in the cradle asleep. I took Malilia in my arms, and kissed her. She said: "Mr John", in Spanish, and fell down dead and lay for one hour. The house filled in a few minutes with people, and I had her in my arms. When she came to herself, she took me round the neck, and fainted away again. She soon recovered. "My child's father! my dear child! He was born the firſt of March, and is four months old." I took her to the hotel with me, and the child in her arms. An hundred people came to see us. I was satisfied the child was my own, and that she had never known any other man. I asked her if she would go to England with me. She said, with all her heart, and all her friends were agreeable if I would marry her. I sent for a priest, and was married directly. She was very merry. Next day a hundred people came to see us go away. She was eighteen years of age, and I thirty-eight. I hired a chaise to take her to Aranjuez and Madrid, as I thought we should stay some days there. We arrived at Aranjuez at dinner, and put up at the hôtel I was at with Sir John Stuart. As the King was at the Escurial, my master went to see what was worth seeing, and set out next day for Madrid, where we stopped two days. I made an agreement with the chaise-driver to take my wife to Toledo, and then to the English hôtel at Lisbon, and I sent a letter to Mr Dewar, the landlord of the same, to get her a passage for England, and to come to me in London, to Berwick Street, Soho.

In France we discharged our men and mules and all our unnecessary luggage, and next day we set out post for Bourdeaux, where we arrived the third day at the English hôtel. My master liked Bourdeaux much. Finding a great many English and Irish gentlemen, he stopped three weeks. He hired a carriage and two servants. At the end of three weeks we set off post for Paris, and arrived, at the end of one week, at the Hôtel de Parc Royal, Rue Faubourg, St Germaine. Here my master intended to stay to amuse himself. He got a chariot and he gave the two servants genteel liveries. My master was a very genteel young man, and handsome. He made a very good appearance wherever he went. On the sixth day of November, in the morning, he said to me : " John, there is five Louis for you." " Sir, what is this for ? " " I give it because this is my birth-day. I am this day twentyone years, and treat the coachman and flamack with what they like to drink." " I will, sir ; and I wish you long life and prosperity, and I hope, sir, that you will have better luck than my laſt maſter, Sir John, had, for on the day he was of age, in the south of France, he loſt a gold watch worth one hundred guineas." About the end of November we left Paris, to go to Brussels. We went to Chantillie, and ſtopped all night. Next morning Mr O'Neil went to see the Palace, the Toartains gardens, hot-house, green-house, and the ſtables, the firſt in the world. Next night we went to the city of Cambrai, and next night to Mons, and next day to Brussels, and put up at the English hôtel. Here was a great many British and Irish gentlemen, and here Mr O'Neil kept his Chriſtmas. Brussels is one of the fineſt places in the world, and there are the fineſt churches. As it was the Chriſtmas time, my maſter and I went to see the churches ornamented and lighted. After three weeks ſtay here, we set out for Ghent, and ſtopped all night ; and next day we went to see the city and the churches ; and the day follow-ing we went to Courtray, and next day to the city of Ypres, where we ſtopped one day ; and next night to Dunkirk. My maſter ſtopped two days, as there were gentlemen he knew. The night before we left

Dunkirk, as I was putting Mr O'Neil to bed, he said :
" I will not go by that poor place Gravelines—I will
go by Boulogne." We went to Boulogne, and ſtopped
two days ; and then to Calais, and took our passage
for Dover, and arrived in London, at Lowe's Hotel, in
January 1779. I went to my lodgings in Berwick
Street to inquire if my wife and child were arrived
from Toledo. When I went in, my landlady asked
me how I did ; and, when the common compliments
were over, I asked her if anyone had called on me.
She answered none, " but there is a foreign letter here
for you four months". When I received the letter I
trembled, leſt some accident had happened to my
wife and child ; but my fears were soon over, when I
opened the letter and read : " My dear husband, you
will be surprised on your arrival in London when you
do not find me and your dear son at your lodgings
at Mrs White's. We are all well, I praise the great
God ; but when I came to my father's door with the
return chaise, when the man told me to be ready by
four next morning, my mother was like a diſtraċted
woman, and said : ' If my only child leaves me, I
certainly cannot live one week ' ; so I was in great
diſtress how to determine. My father came in, and
between us he was very uneasy ; so he went for his
cousin, Mr Logaro, the maſter of the Hôtel de Naples,
where I firſt saw you ; so when he came, my father
asked his opinion, how his daughter should do, concerning going to London. ' If my daughter goes, I
shall lose my wife, and I should be sorry never to see

my daughter again. Now cousin, give me your advice.' 'I am sorry to see the distress you are in. I would have Malilia stop with her mother, and I believe her husband is a man of good character by what I have seen of his behaviour and by his being here twice with gentlemen of fortune. Write to him the distress your wife is in to part with her daughter, and, if he would come to Toledo, we can do better for him than his living in service and going round the country; so, my dear husband, if you will be condescending to this request, we shall be all happy. If you do not choose to come, let me know your commands, and I will fulfil them if it was at the peril of my life: let me have an answer as soon as possible. I believe, when you see me again, I shall be the mother of two children. Your son is a fine boy; everyone here calls him 'the little Englishman'. I shall conclude, and every day I shall think of the letter which I expect to receive from you. Pray, my dear John Macdonald, if it be possible, come to Toledo. So no more from your

Loving wife unto death,

Malilia Macdonald."

August 22, 1778.

When I came back to the hôtel, my master's father had just arrived from Dublin to receive his son; he said to me: "Are you my son's servant?" "Sir, I am Mr O'Neil's servant; he is gone out, and he will be in soon." Next day I determined in my own mind

247

what to do. After the gentlemen were dressed, I went down to Wapping to inquire if there were any ship going to Spain. At the St Andrew's I found a ship was to sail in three weeks for Bilboa in the province of Biscay, in the north of Spain. I said that would answer my purpose; so I took my passage. Captain Jenkins was the Captain's name. After one week in town, the gentlemen were preparing to set off for Ireland. One morning my master asked me if I would go to Ireland with him. I thanked him, and I answered : " I am going to Spain with a gentleman, and, as your father has two servants here, you can do without me : the butler will take care of your things, and I am much obliged to you for all favours. I never enjoyed more happiness than with you." My master paid me off, and his father sent the butler for me to come into the parlour, and he made me a present of a twenty-pound bank-note, and next day they set off for Dublin. I sold all my things off, and made ready to take my passage to Bilboa. We all got on board, and in one month from the Thames we arrived at Bilboa. As we were preparing to go on shore, I looked back and said to myself : " Farewell Great Britain and Ireland, if I should or should not see you again." I stopped at Bilboa one day. I found several people going to Burgos city, some merchants and some seafaring people, to see their relations. I had one mule to ride and another for my baggage and for the man to ride that was to bring back the mules. When we left Bilboa two stages we came into a road

I had travelled twice before. The people knew me on the road. The company were all very civil; therefore we travelled with great pleasure. In three days we arrived at Burgos, and stopped at our old house. Here all the company left us but one going to Segovia. We had fresh mules as before, and arrived in four days. Here I waited one day to have an opportunity to be one in a return chaise to Madrid, which was rather more agreeable to ride, than on a mule. We set out three of us in the chaise and everything was very agreeable. We walked on foot over the mountains and hills. We came to Madrid in three days, where I stopped two nights with a relation of my wife's : then I set off for Toledo, by a return coach. We went through Aranjuez, and arrived at Toledo at my father-in-law's. My wife was brought to bed, in a week after, of another boy. I said to myself : " The Macdonalds grow in Spain." My wife was overjoyed to see me, and I was glad to see my wife and children. My wife's father and mother and Mr Logaro were very glad to see me come amongst them. Numbers of their friends came to see me. Next day I went to Mr Logaro's, at the Hôtel de Naples, and there I was employed to my satisfaction. So now I end the history of my travels.

INDEX

INDEX

INDEX

INDEX

INDEX